STRENGTHENING *the* DEFENCES

STRENGTHENING *the* DEFENCES

BE STRONG IN THE LORD

TREVOR O. TURNER

Copyright © 2019 by Trevor O. Turner.

Library of Congress Control Number: 2019907478

PAPERBACK: 978-1-7332264-0-0
EBOOK: 978-1-7332264-1-7

Ordering Information:

For orders and inquiries, please contact:
1-888-404-1388
www.goldtouchpress.com
book.order@goldtouchpress.com

Printed in the United States of America

CONTENTS

DEDICATION

I dedicate this book to the glory of God and trust that all who read it will receive its message and will themselves be strengthened to continue living a triumphant life in Christ. I do hope that the amount so helped will be copious.

ACKNOWLEDGEMENT

I acknowledged those wonderful people below who gave me the endorsements and wrote the forward and helped in so many ways.

Forward by: Dr. Irving Pisarek.
Endorsements by: Pastor Adams, Juanita Brown and Stephanie White.
Vanessa Huayta-Turner my daughter and my in house IT personnel.

To all of you, I gratefully acknowledge your help and support. May the Lord continue to bless you all abundantly!

FORWARD

As his Chiropractor, I have known Trevor Turner since the fall of 2003. He was referred to me by his wife Maria and both are blessed with 14 grandchildren, the youngest being only a few months old.

Having known Trevor for the past 14 years, I can attest that this fine compassionate accomplished and physically fit senior citizen should be a "poster boy" for others even half his age. He is truly a person that constantly seeks to improve his inner self along with the physical. He works out regularly at the gym and cycles several kilometers, weather permitting.

He is the fourth child of twelve children and migrated to Canada in 1969. He has accumulated a wealth of work experiences over the years and has traveled extensively. He has had many Church relatedpositions over the years and continues to work as a lay Evangelist. This book is his newest. In it, he reinforces his own faith and uses it as an evangelizing tool to win others to the Lord.

It is written especially to edify and encourage the Christian to walk humbly and uprightly in a confused and rapacious world. The thrust is to encourage the reader to learn to recognize Biblical truths from false and spurious teachings. This book is full of Biblical passages to support every claim which he makes in support of his stance. He hopes his book will encourage the "redeemed" to live as "overcomers" and not as "defeatists" as so many are living. This is his platform which he prays will reach the audience he would not ordinarily reach personally.

Trevor prays he will have the joy of meeting some soul in heaven who has read his book.

In closing, my wife Hilda and I have been truly blessed to have met Trevor and his wife Maria. We believe that there is a "greater power" constantly at work that has brought the Turners into our office domain to administer the inner 'healing natural powers' of modern Chiropractic care.

I am humbled to have been bestowed the honour of writing this "Forward" and trust that 'you' the reader will gain the truthful knowledge in the message that Trevor presents in his newest literary work; "Strengthening the Defences."

Dr. Irving Pisarek, Chiropractor
Toronto, Ontario
Canada.
Dated: August 2017.
Strengthening the Defences

CHAPTER 1

BREAKING FREE

Dear reader, this letter is an invitation for you to read and digest all that is written in this book for it will fortify and strengthen you for the journey ahead which although might not be onerous presently, nevertheless, needs great courage and strength to march on to victory and to make a triumphant entry into the Lord's presence. I encourage you to own this book and to read every word that is written on its pages and you will undoubtedly come out a better person at the end. You will quite pleasantly be as victorious in your battle here on earth as Joshua or Lord Nelson. You will undoubtedly come out a victor.

Breaking clean from certain habits and customs is a reasonable thing to do and most times it is the only sensible thing to do. A person who is double minded is a fickle person and much is not expected of them. That person will not weather the storm in difficult times. Undoubtedly they will succumb to the prevailing wind and will not have the fortitude or rectitude to stand their ground and act out their convictions. They will vacillate and might even deny their very Lord; such a person will sell their soul and not realize it. Conviction is a person's honour and it will take them places; it will buttress their character and fortify them. Conviction builds character and character makes a person. The person is nothing neither more nor less than their character. A person is not judged by their appearance, their physique, their wealth but by their character. That is how we judge someone, simply by their lives; the kind of life they lived. That is the measure of a person, their life and not their wealth. Is that life wholly profane or is it a Godly one? This is the question. How will we exist, sojourn and eventually be remembered. No one but us can write that last chapter of our lives. If we come to that realization, then we would better start writing all things salubrious now.

John Newton, a slave trader, profligate and a drunkard, revelled in that life; met God and wrote a last chapter of his life that we all remember. He made an about turn at Calvary and that made all the difference in his life afterwards which in turn has affected the rest of us for good also. He counted it an amazing act that God should look upon him, a great sinner and has mercy upon him. He expressed his thankfulness in many hymns, one of which is: *Amazing Grace.* His life before conversion would not have been worth remembering; it would not have been worth mentioning. It would have receded in oblivion but something happened which gave him abundant life and a purpose for living; he found the Saviour and had a miraculous transformation. From then on, he embraced life as purposeful and enchanting and went on to live a remarkable and influential life. The last chapter in his book was guided by the hand of God.

2 Why is it an anomaly when one shines as an honourable person these days? It is because the fences have been broken down and all the infectious conditions have crawled in. Few there are who will stand for right and integrity. Few there are who will see the wrong and seek to denounce it and stand up for righteousness. Generally, honour is no longer a strong enough claim on our lives to live and to die for.

A man takes a job and for whatever reason, calculated the cost of the job wrongly, shorting himself in the end but nevertheless, he does not stop halfway on the job, he finishes it at a loss to himself. Why! Because his honour is at stake! A cowhand was given a job to herd some cattle to the slaughter house in the good old days; before trucking and railroading became the means of transporting livestock and it took him far longer than he had anticipated and with more hardships than he had imagined, yet he persevered and came out honourable. He delivered. One reporter asked him why he persisted and his reply was: "I gave my word." A man, a woman stays in a marriage which no longer works, yet he or she stays and do their best because they are honourable people; they will rather suffer the deprivation of a good marriage than to walk away and let down the other partner. Those individuals have a principle by which they live and pattern their lives. We will respect them and honour them. Everyone loves a principled person and even if we are not principled ourselves, yet we know we can trust such a person.

Life is too short to be disorganized. We need to break free from encumbrances which weigh us down, preventing us from running the race which is set before us. The sooner we get our act together, the sooner we can hit the road to living a good life, an abundant life, an honourable life; *an exuberant* life.

We rely on such people and even trust them as leaders or emulate them as examples who are strong enough to make a clean break from old ties, bad habits and a life of degradation. The couple, who marries, makes that commitment and breaks unfettered from their parents' home. They do not leave somethings still at the parents' home, hoping to go back someday to live there again. Not at all, they throw all their weight in the new relationship and hope for the best. Each partner is expecting total commitment and expenditure of energy into the new home from the other. Success can only be expected and experienced with such an attitude and indulgence. In essence, we love to see maturity in a person, Christian or not.

When the eagle determines that it is time for her chicks to leave the nest, having served them from birth to that point, she simply breaks up the nest and forces them out. The bear also, at a certain age runs the cubs away from home or the den. These are forcibly exists. I would to God that the Christian could be weaned off the world just as forcibly without recourse. We certainly would learn and thrive better than we do at the moment. Invariably however, we and that goes for most of us have developed an attitude of uncertainty; one where we are not quite sure that it is going to work out so we linger still for some time in the world. We simply have not burned our bridges to the old world. We have not "*broken clean*" from the old world. To thrive and prosper in the new life, we must break clean from the old, or else we will forever be that pathetic person who is trying to play a part that we are no longer suited for. We see them and we know them. We ourselves know that to be triumphant and happy we

3 must break free from this world and its system. Paul warns us in Romans 12:2: "*And be not conformed to this world: but be ye transformed by the renewing of your mind, that ye may prove what is that good, and acceptable, and perfect, will of God.*"

This is proving ground, we cannot know and we will not know the power of God until we break free from the world and its allurements. We must be sold out to God completely. Our Christianity must be a contrast to the world. I have come into circumstances where I am told that I would not be a bad person if it were not for my religion. It is my religion therefore which gets in the way.

We have become sounding brass and tickling cymbals and send out a false message to the world when our actions are perceived as false. One man after watching another who was a man of God lived for years said if God could not keep that churchgoer, then God, would not be able to save him who was a wreck. May God help us to take stock daily and even minutely so that we bring honour and not dishonour to His name. We attract and not repulse.

We are on the subject of breaking clean or making a clean break and I will use this example in my own life to drive home this point. When I migrated to Canada from Jamaica in 1969, I applied as a family of seven and we all got our passports and came as one family. The house which I owned or built in Jamaica was rented out and strange enough, I never collected a cent for rent. I had to send money to take care of all the expenses including a small mortgage. One friend told me here not to sell it when I mentioned to him of my intention to settle here in Canada but I did not listen to him and in 1971, I went back and sold it and bought one here. Another friend said to me, Trevor, do not break ties altogether but I was determined to break loose and start afresh here. To cut a long story short, in spite of hardships and setbacks, I survived and prospered and I am happy I did. There is always an old and a new and we must separate them especially when we are dealing with eternal matters which brings with it eternal and irreversible consequences. I cannot stress the importance of this fact any clearer than I have done here.

A flashback now to many earlier years; as a matter fact, going back to when I just finished school and started to work. That was way back in 1956. My first job was with Bauxite Company as a records clerk. The school we grew up in was run by the Moravian church. One evening the Minister and his wife came to me and ask if I wanted a job to teach at the school, of course at that time I was not looking for a job, I had my well-paying job already with the Bauxite Company. The reason they sought me out was because at the final exams, I helped the Minister's wife(they were not married then of course) with her math and she passed her examination, which of course put her in my debt.

Another time I had to make a decision between an Architectural Drafting position over a Life Insurance one. Further to that and before coming to Canada, my sister got me a job in the Bahamas where she and my brother were working. While processing the papers for going over the Bahamas, I received an envelope from the Canadian embassy where I had applied for entry to Canada some time before and instead of the Bahamas I came to Canada. These are some of the instances where I had to make choices between two places and whether or not I made the right choice, only God knows but on the matter of whether to follow Christ or remain in the world; I knew and still know that I made the

4 correct one by choosing to follow Him. This choice of following Christ have eternal consequences and there can be no reversal of consequence if I had taken the wrong turn as many have and entered eternity. Following Christ is never a bad choice; it is always ever the best choice one can make.

Having therefore, realized that the choice I made was the correct and the most satisfying one, I urge men and women everywhere and every time to make that decision. It is the only one which pays everlasting dividends. The dividends keep on coming and increases as the days and years roll on. The great climax will be seeing our blessed Saviour face to face who died on Calvary's cross for us. That is one decision one will never ever regret that they had made. It is the one which is forever gratifying, paying benefits for all eternity. The reason for the choice of following Jesus Christ grows stronger and stronger as the years roll on for me and for everyone I am sure who seriously throw themselves into the fray. There is no greater reason for living, as we move from life into eternity than to be a bond slave of the Master. It is indeed the only reason for our existence. It is like coming out at the other end of the pool alive after falling in and then you know that you have had your years of painstakingly learning to swim validated then and there. Your live was literally in your own hands. You managed to save your life by the action which you had taken over the many years. You overcame the arduous task of learning to swim which not only added another dimension to your life but saved it in the end.

Dear brother, dear sister push on through the day, through the night and push on through the rain and the sunshine but push on. There is a bright light and a glorious day at the end of the tunnel, and at the end of the hardships and disappointment but it is there. There will be no disappointment.

A glorious eternity; one free from all the hardships, disappointments, strife and striving and failings and whatever else besets us down here is awaiting us with our Lord and Saviour Jesus Christ when we take the time to lay it all at the cross and follow Him. Following Him calls for wholehearted commitment and devotion and nothing less. We cannot be of two opinions; we must take a stand for or against Him.

Some will say that they are not against Him but do not take a stand on His side, then you are indeed against Him for He said: "You cannot serve two masters." Matthew 6:24. You cannot be of two opinions. You must take a definite stand on one side or the other. James tells us that a double minded man is unstable in all his ways. James 1:8. Stability is quite simply security. Security is in Christ Jesus when we make Him lord. You will not know that security until difficulties reigns in your life, and then you will have a shoulder to lean on. It is then that you will know the meaning of trusting Christ. He never fails; not now, not ever. He is the creator of all things and the redeemer of mankind. Trust Him.

I support many charitable organizations and if it is revealed to me that anyone that has an element of anti-God in it, I will cease to support that one because notwithstanding the many good that is inherent in it, one evil would be counterproductive to the cause which I am passionate about. I cannot give my money to a cause that I am fighting to eradicate. It is the same with me in worship; I will support a Church where Christ is honoured, that is; I will throw my heart into that work. If there is alignment to untruth and it is known to me, I will not support such a work.

5 *Never, never, be disconsolate*

When Jesus was on earth and during His last days before the crucifixion, He warned that He was leaving and the disciples were concerned for they wanted to be with him always. They could not bear to lose Him; they would surely be disconsolate especially how they had come to rely upon Him for those three and a half years. They had become one big family. He had become part of their very existence as they travelled the dusty roads of Palestine preaching and teaching and working miracles. He was their friend and great teacher and they looked forward to the day when He would be king and they in turn would be part of the hierarchy. That is looking forward to a glorious future. These were men still bound and held by the cosmos, they were earthly or carnal. They would soon enter into another dimension, however, the spiritual; after His death, resurrection and ascension. Their lives and outlook on life would be totally transformed then. Now the excitement after such an event could not be contained as they began to be effective witnesses. They became bold witnesses after receiving the promised gift of the Holy Spirit.

In our time, we occasionally come across inconsolable people when they come into circumstance, such as suddenly losing a loved one. The breadwinner is suddenly cut off and those remaining cannot begin to see how they will ever exist without such a one. In all of this sudden loss, the biggest disconsolation is to know, that for that person, eternity is uncertain. That uncertainty brings the biggest distress, knowing that there is a future for which the departed had not prepared. That is distress magnified a thousand times. I remember some years ago a girl was shot by accident downtown at a: *"Just for deserts bar"* and she was elegized by her mother as a church going and beautiful girl, yet she cried: "I wonder where she is now." There was not the consolation that she was where she strived to be while she lived. Is this part of our worship, shallow and superficial; having no certainty as to where we are heading? We can be sure of the road ahead, we must be sure of the road we are on.

Amid the anxiety of the disciples and upon hearing of His impending departure, Jesus gave them some assurances that all would be well. He said to them in john 14:1: "Let not your heart be troubled: ye believe in God, believe also in me." Verse 27: "Peace I leave with you, my peace I give unto you: not as the world giveth… Let not your heart be troubled neither let it be afraid." This is confidence personified given by the Master Himself. Jesus made that statement to the disciples of His day and it rings true to every believer throughout the ages and down to us presently. We as believers must do more than believe in God; we must believe God. We must exercise faith to the degree where we experience His power in our lives, be it for healing or a financial crisis. Whatever it is that we want legitimately, we should ask in confidence believing that we will receive it. This is the believer's positionin God. We no longer approach our Father in fear, doubting as we ask but we can ask with confidence and have peace in asking. Now are we children and heirs of the Kingdom. We are adopted into the Family of God and legally are a part of the family. The poorest of us inherit equally as all others. This is now our standing before God.

6 We are, therefore, not disconsolate nor can we be, for under God we have been made partakers of the divine inheritance. We are now heirs and joint heirs with Christ Jesus our Lord. Romans 8:17. We must allow that reality to sink in and settle in our psyche permanently. We do not doubt and wonder what will become of us but we know what has become of us. We belong to the household of faith and now are we part of that Royal Priesthood and the Holy Nation, how can we then continue to live as indigent dwellers? When we do, we bring dishonour to His name and are literally squandering His resources. We are simply not making the best use of our talents, some of us are literally burying our talents and we know the outcome of such behaviours.

I states explicitly: "But ye are a chosen generation, a royal priesthood, an holy nation, a peculiar people; that ye should show forth the praises of Him who hath called you out of darkness into His marvelous light." We must always ruminate upon this verse of Scripture to fully know our standing in Christ Jesus, that is, of course, all who profess His Name.

To the person who has not yet trusted Christ, I am convinced that if that person ceases everything they are doing or are engaged in right now which has a worldly ring to it and bow before the Almighty and turn their backs on it, they will be amply rewarded. There is nothing too splendid that we cannot give up and mourn the loss for Christ's sake. God has promised it and we the believers attest to it that life on this side of the coin is richer and more resplendent than anything, anywhere, bar none. Christ not only promises a good life, He delivers it. Great men and women have stopped dead in their tracks and left their lucrative careers to follow Jesus of Nazareth and never looked back. They have given themselves to helping and caring and preaching to the poor and needy of this world and are well fulfilled by doing so. These have broken loose from their careers to give to the Lord that which they cannot lose. Fulfilment and consolation only lie in Christ Jesus and in Him alone. His consolation far outweighs anything this world has to offer despite the behaviours of some of us. All the glitter and gold of this world pale in comparison to possessing Jesus Christ. His presence is the living water which when taken quenches every thirst and longing. He is fulfilment personified. Need I say more?

I know a woman who after losing a daughter to cancer locked herself in her bathroom for two years. She could not be consoled; she was totally heartbroken and many years later that same woman lost a son and she had to be hospitalized, so deep was her sorrow. If we know the Lord, things are different in our affairs because we have an advocate with whom we can communicate and bring our problems to. We know that he knows everything we will go through long before this world begun and will see His children through every circumstances of life. He will comfort us through those difficult times. He will, because He has promised it. God longs to be our comforter if we would but come to Him. He is our father and not only tells us that He loves us but showers us with His best gifts. Our principal gift is His son Jesus Christ. If such act of love is shown, how can any believer be poor and linger in uncertainty? It is shameful to say the least. A defeatist attitude should and must be foreign to us permanently. We simply cannot live as the redeemed as though we have no available and accessible resource. We must live as rich people, drawing on the available resources of God.

7 In spite of adversity, failure, heartaches, disappointments and whatever else comes our way, when we follow Christ we must look on them as the seeds for greater growth and blessings. An abundant life is ours and not the debilitating issues that are common to us. We must show forth His power in our lives and that power makes us overcomers. No longer are we underdogs and subservient dwellers but full-fledged masters, not hoping to enter into some future blessings but are in those blessings now.

Isaiah 45:3 reads: "And I will give thee the treasure of darkness, and hidden riches of secret places, that thou mayest know, that I the Lord … am the God of Israel." The lord will do what pleases Him to get His purposes done; He can build a wall if necessary or use a spider's web as one but in every or any event He is sufficient. He is not just sufficient for our needs but more than sufficient. Is this preceding statement only just words being penned or is it true for us as Christians? If Christ be anything to us, He has to be everything. We must not rest, until His love and truth be the consuming passions of our souls. We must be immersed in Christ totally to experience victory in our lives. In secular events we know how to equip ourselves in order to succeed; we must immerse ourselves totally to come out victorious, then why do we treat our Christianity with less expediency and fervency? We watch the ball game or whatever game in place of attending the services in the house of God. We do not acquaint ourselves with the things in Christian circles but we are quite proficient in the events of this world. Are we then feasting on the husks of life, like the Prodigal son and neglecting our father's table?

If climbing the ladder was the way into heaven, many of us would only be at the first rung, when by age and length of time in the church many should be at the last rung, ready to enter the door. This is the way I see it anyhow, more interest is paid to the sinking ship than launching the lifeboat to get off. Some are still below deck scrambling to save a few trinkets instead of being busy getting into the lifeboat.

Why am I writing this? Is it to fill the pages or is this my passion also. It is my passion to enter into the blessedness of His love and power. I want to live the life of a victor and one of power with men and with God. This is my prayer that my faith will not waver in any circumstance, be it a dark and suffocating experience or a simple one. I want to know that what He says he will do is what He intends to do for me Trevor Turner. This is my consolation, that I know, that my God reigns over all my circumstances. This value is intrinsic in serving my Lord and any lesser claim on His word would be invective to say the least. The Lord has spoken, let us then believe Him. The mind of God toward us is not shrouded in secrecy; it is suffused throughout the pages of the Bible for our edification. Since we have fallen behind, far behind in our fervency, it is time for us to fall on our knees and ask for forgiveness for our unbelief because we sin in our inactions and impotence.

Stop vacillating now

Jesus states in Matthew 6:24: "No man can serve two masters: for either he will hate the one and love 8 the other: …Ye cannot serve God and mammon." It is that simple, it is the law of balance. It is either you go up or go down. We are never in a state of inertia. There is always a pull on us and we must yield to one pull or the other. Jesus being God knows which master we ought to serve and He invites us to follow Him and not lose out at the end. He loves us and is not willing that any should perish but that all should come to repentance, nevertheless, we are given a choice and it is up to us. He pleads with us to come but few heed the call. Each person wants to have dominion and control over their own life as long as they live. The feeble eighty and ninety year old person does not want to leave their house, they want to die there. They have to be dragged out like Lot; so attached they are to the brick and mortar. We want to cling to this old world which is of diminishing value and we do not know it. This attitude is not only held by the secular but also by those of the household of God. Some are just so happy and contented to live out their lives in whatever state they are in, in whatever religion they were brought up in, regardless of whether it is doing anything for them or not; regardless of whether it will give them a life off when the trumpet sounds or not.

Many do not want to be disturbed. I have encountered them; they want to be left alone. One man said to me: "I am contented with my religion, I hope you are too" that was his response to the Gospel or to a tract. Do not tell them that the sky is falling, they will not take shelter. So they don't want to be disturbed, for life is good and rightly so but then what at death? Or after death? We must face our Maker then and how will we plead then? If we did it our way in life then in death we are on our own which is a sad state to be in, for the word *"Depart"* will be our command. Not well done or welcome. They will have gotten their reward or reached their destination because of the road which they took. The plight of their decision while living will have come upon them and hit them with such realismbut they will be impotent to do anything about it. They cannot now even ask for mercy for it will have been too late. While they lived, they squandered their inheritance and now they are left destitute.

At such a time God cannot wink at their ignorance because they have had the light, His son Jesus Christ all throughout their lives. Mahatma Han Ghandi said: "All around me is darkness and I am praying for the light." This is the saddest commentary on this world today, is that the light has come and we are still groping in darkness. It is sad to say the least. Many do see and hear but they ignore the call as useless and disturbing. They continue walking in the darkness which takes them to the destiny of their choice. "Hell." How shall they escape if they neglect so great a Salvation. Christ dying on the Cross for their redemption meant nothing to them. Their involvement was placed in something else, they were misplaced in things; things of diminishing value.

God does not force us to surrender to Him. One man I witnessed to, asked me: "Why did God make us so we could rebel or disobey Him? Why didn't He make us so we would have to obey Him?" I told him that when I get to heaven I will ask the Lord but he would better be there to get his answer. We would be robots, programmed to serve God if we did not have a mind of our own. Here we are now as free agents reasoning that if we were robots then none would go to hell. We can reason thus far and yet we have the chance to choose the right path and we desire to go in the opposite direction. It is willful and deliberate rebellion. I will not have this man to rule over me they say. I want to remain free 9 to indulge in my sinful habits; here is where I am happiest. In essence, we do like choices even if we make the wrong ones more often than we would like.

As we consider our lot, there is a strong sentiment which pulls us and influences our choices, and that pull is love. Basic to our character is love; we love to love something or somebody and as such we must express that love either to self, above the Creator or to the Creator above self. Some love the world and make no excuse for loving it. They must have it all as it is offered as a panacea. This is the state of the unregenerate person. On the contrary, the regenerate person learns to love His Redeemer now more than themselves and possessions. This is not an unusual occurrence for where your treasure is, there will your heart be also.

Our hearts will have to undergo a radical transformation to shift our lovefrom things or possessions and self to God. By "Ipso Facto" that very act or transformation of our hearts, we have now been given the spirit of love and power and a sound mind. We rejoice now in a new beginning and delight in a hopeful end. We have been reconciled to our Redeemer through the Blood of our crucified Lord. We delight in serving and loving Him instead of things and ourselves. We are reckoned dead to the world but alive unto Christ. This is the reality of our existence and the essence of our standing in this life. We stand strong and firm on the Rock of our salvation to the exclusion of everything else. Our hope is no longer in possessions and our intellects but in the Almighty God and His word and why not. Wise men still seek Jesus, will you add your name to that list?

CHAPTER 2

PURSUE TO FIND AND TO HOLD

You have read, you have listened, you have lived, and you have observed; but you have not assimilated the truth in its entirety. There is still lingering in your heart some doubt and disbelief. There is a richness of being, that we can or must achieve when our expectations and our connections are aligned to the Truth. There is a truth that is neither yours nor mine; it is handed down by the Great Creator. The power that be, without question, absolute and true. We vacillate between truth and half-truths or as we hear nowadays: Alternative Truth. We live in a world where we are well informed about more things than our forefathers ever dreamt of and yet we live by lies. If we are not telling them we are swallowing them as they are told to us. We delude ourselves into thinking that what or all we hear is veracious and worthwhile and wholesome and satisfying and will fulfill like no other. That the animal advertised is destined to get us somewhere and to dispense the happiness we dreamt of. Be this vehicle of conveyance a material good or a religious involvement, something captivating is presented and we are apt to

10 embrace it. Such is our makeup and we are compelled to engage ourselves because there is a void, a vacuum to be filled and our wellbeing hangs on such engagements. We might easily

agree then that we cannot stand still; we have to be fully engaged in one thing or another. Engagement is not only necessary; it is paramount for our very survival. We pity the person who has no form of engagement. The disengagement with life, breeds boredom and boredom brings ruin. For any growth to sprout and flourish, engagement must be embraced. Stagnation and rot are the end results of inertia. We cannot stand still, we must be engaged at whatever level we can but engagement is a must. There is therefore no real rest for us in earnest. The only possible rest there is for us, is to rest in the love of God through faith in Him. As Saint Augustine states: "Our souls are restless until they rest in God." It is so because we were made to worship God and find ourselves in Him.

There is a time and a place for everything under the sun says Ecclesiastes. There is a time in ones life to seek and to find God, for He is ready to receive you but there is a time also when you have gambled with that opportunity and lost, for you had waited too long. All things are not in our hands ultimately but God's and that time may come when he closes the door. God is no man's debtor and as such He is not obliged to answer us whenever we call. It's been many men's experiences that when they call upon the Lord He turns a deaf ear because they spurned Him for too long. If that heart remains stubborn and recalcitrant for too long in their ways, there is danger ahead. Today He says, if you hear my voice harden not your heart. This is even my pleading with you dear reader, respond to the calling now for He is calling. He is calling even through these pages.

God is our eventual resting place and He provides rest from our wonderings perhaps but definitely rest for our weary souls. If we place our trust in Him, at the strend of our sojourn here on earth then we are welcomed home into His presence and rest. To be in Christ is a glorious realization. There is no other state like it. Those who have not embraced Him will forever be floundering and restless and purposeless. He is the Christians guiding star and light. He is the truth by which we live and grow and prosper. He is the compass by which we chart our course. This reality is planted in our souls. Yes! We can now cultivate a beautiful garden inwardly when we put our trust in Christ.

The world as we see it gives hints of being a suitable host for a flourishing and restful life but when scrutinized closely the tantalizing promises of joy and happiness turns out to be every time a taunting mirage. The joy we seek is not substantive; it is transient and fleeting, a mirage indeed. Who can doubt that this is so? There is no gimmick or trick or technique that is sustaining to bring about the happiness we seek. Happiness cannot be found in material

11 possessions solely to the neglect of the eternal dimension in our thoughts, if so, we remain unfulfilled and shallow; always searching for more.

Did we just say that happiness is not found in material things? Let us check it out Biblically. In Isaiah 2:8 we read: "Their land also is full of idols; they worship the work of their own hands, that which their own fingers have made:" Idols are things which we worship and if Israel wasfull of idols then, how much more are our land today. We rent storage spaces when our houses cannot contain our abundance and set up bins outside to accommodate the excesses. We are the biggest idol worshippers of all times. We spend our wealth on monster houses to house a family of three and four and the list is endless because we are never satisfied, our appetite for goods is insatiable and in the end our lives vanishes like a tale that was told and that is all because one has not found the fountain of living water that satisfies. That fountain is available.

"There is a fountain filled with blood drawn from Emmanuel's veins and sinners plunge beneath that flood lose all his guilty and stain." William Cowper. Help is only a prayer away dear reader. God has not cast away the sinner altogether and he pleads with us constantly, thus it is written: "*...For all this His anger is not turned away, but His hand is stretched out still.*" Isaiah 10:4. God's anger abides in duality with His mercy and as such He remains a merciful God; not willing that any should perish but that all should come to repentance.

There is a fallacy that we are the captains of our own ships and we can steer it into the haven of rest as we please but herein lie the root of our error. The peace which brings happiness is the tranquility of order which Saint Augustine terms: "The perfectly ordered and harmonious enjoyment of God and of one another in God." In simple terms, outside the sphere of God, we will not or cannot even enjoy the fellowship and harmony we should and can have with our fellow human beings. The first principle then for the *Good Life* is to accept the sovereignty of God and relinquish the reins of your life to Him now. We are co-captains at best and were never intended to be Captains in our own rights. We have some navigating abilities but for the obtrusive places we cannot guide the craft securely, we must then hand over to the Captain fully. We must come to accept some basic principles as truths or we will keep on floundering throughout our lives.

There was a time when we lingered in the valley of indecision and truth was of little concern to us but today we rejoice in only one thing and that is the Truth. 1 Corinthians 13: 6. "Rejoiceth not in inequity but rejoiceth in the truth." Oh wondrous grace which has brought us thus far, causing us to rejoice in this splendid virtue. Truth is the dynamic in our lives which tells us right from wrong and good from evil if you will. Truth is the anvil on which all unrighteousness is crushed. The ignorant stumbles over it and the learned struggles with it. Little wonder God

12 shakes us regularly so we can take stock and get back to basics. So often we wonder off on a tangent which leads us away from the centre of righteousness. Truth is the all-encompassing word which liberates us and sets us free. Finding truth is the ultimate prize in life.

Jesus prayed these words to His Father for us: "Sanctify them through thy truth: thy word is truth." John 17:17. In light of this statement how can we say then that the word of God depends upon ones interpretation? One should not seek to put their own twist upon the message of the Bible but simply to believe it. This is what sets the Christian apart from the crowd, this is what sets us apart from the pretenders and that is the truth of God's word. As Biblicists, we study the word of Truth and know it as God's dogma. We know it and seek to live by it.

Christians are a community of believers with a hope and a destination. When we were born again through faith in Jesus Christ we became a part of the generation of Jesus Christ. We all have an earthly standing at birth. Our generation is defined by our surnames but now we are given a new surname through the second birth. We are now one big family? Whatever station or origin we hail from; we are under the same umbrella and can embrace each other as brothers and sisters. If I were to state this as a fact one might easily throw it aside as presumptuous talk but read the following from the author of our salvation.

In john 17:21 Jesus speaking to His Father said: "That they all may be one; as thou, Father, art in me, and I in thee, that they also may be one in us: ..." This statement is a little hard to digest and assimilate and who am I to try to dissect this passage but I will try nevertheless. In other parts of Scripture Jesus wants to make it plain that we are not servants but His friends. Hear Him again in John 15:15: "Henceforth I call you not servants; for the servant knoweth not what his lord doeth: but I have called you friends; for all things that I have heard of my Father I have made known unto you." We are in the inner circle and are not fighting and craning out necks to see and know what is going on, we already know. We have been given the manual, the Bible which reveals the mind of God to Us. We know by aligning ourselves with the Word and submerging ourselves in it. The word is the truth and reveals unto us all that we need to know. How is it then, that some of us are living like outsiders and ignorant men and women. That must not be. I urge every brother or sister to stay informed.

Recently I saw a documentary of men and women living in a section of Philadelphia and they simply live by the needle and die by it. It is a place where it was mentioned that they come from all over the country to die literally. They OD on drugs. These people have lost their purpose for living; they have lost the zest for life. Many could not be coaxed into living in a palace; they are the living dead in reality. For all intents and purposes, these people have ceased to live, they

13 have 84ing. It would be harsh to criticise these poor souls, as we ourselves could be a part of the very mix we deem so pathetic. We know that if we had not seen the light ourselves, we too would be dwelling in darkness and even as we dwell in the light there are times when the darkness seems close, too close; almost enveloping and suffocating us. As Charlie Brown says: "It is not that there are not problems, it is only because he chose to be happy while he keeps smiling." This attitude and stance should be the Christian's motto; reigning above all and every circumstances, no matter how black, remembering that we are more than conquerors through Jesus who loved us.

Of course, this reigning and winning attitude is a stark contrast to the rest of the world and yet somewhere, sometimes, we all figure in that category or equation where we suffer from the doldrums. We too or most of us do live as though we are in the camp of the living dead though we have been resurrected and given the new life. We live a disconnected life from our Maker, we are like the branch that is cut off and effectively has lost its life giving source and will not survive. Many of us are adrift and most certainly will flounder if not resuscitated. If we do not hear again John! or Mary! "Come forth" as Jesus called forth to Lazarus we shall remain as dead people. With the genius in us, we drift and manage to survive and invent new gods to hang on to and occupy ourselves with but without full commitment to God, the All Mighty God, we will not be totally happy or fulfilled. We need to be compensated for having passed this way, so take a number and get in line. The offer is true and substantive and irrevocable, take it as promised and begin to serve the Lord with gladness and act as sober personnel of the kingdom.

Some, because of coincidences survived the shipwreck and attribute the rescue to the help of the gods. Then in the process it becomes a transactional affair thereafter. I appease the gods and they look after me. And in time we build monuments to the gods where we can have a place to worship. We must appease our gods and yet these gods are as substantive as a balloon against a pin. The gods we make cannot help us, they are impotent at best; they are in name only but lack any power to help. There is none besides Him. All throughout the Bible the saints testify that there is none other with power besides Jehovah. Many who were antagonistic to Him have come to the realization that his claim is valid. Whether He is acknowledged or not, however, the veracity that He is God still stands and can in no way be diminished by the skeptics.

In 2 Samuel 7:22 David acknowledged before the Lord: "Wherefore thou art great, O Lord God: for there is none like thee…" This is the believer's adulations and praises too; there is none like Thee. We no longer vacillate between two opinions; we no longer believe that there is

14 no one but Thee, for it is now our own experiences that that statement is so. We acknowledge this truth experientially. We are now possessors of the promises. We literally have and hold the things which were promised. Things such as eternal life, an inheritance that fades not away, working on a clean slate, all past and future trespasses and sins washed away. Like Abraham, our faith too is counted for righteousness before God. We stand forgiven, righteous and blameless. No record of any offence can be found now, nor will be found for all eternity against us. How very comforting is this? The one thing that can come between us and our God is sin and we are now sinless, we are in the clear. We have a balanced book and we have been reconciled to our Maker for the first time in our existence and this is something to sing

about. No longer are we slaves to this sin cursed earth. We are as good as having left this earth and are living somewhere else. Much can be said about that of course but that is our heritage and we must now adapt to this new reality. We are no longer of this world but pilgrims and sojourners making our exits through it.

Let us start showing off our new lifestyle now. Living in a manner that contradicts the world's standard. Never more must we exhibit the rapacious nature which once possessed and harassed us. Let our great gain be that which is spoken of in the Bible. Let it be godliness with contentment. 1 Timothy 6:6. Have you ever noticed a baby in a stroller with no shoes, no worries in the world; as relaxed as cooked spaghetti. That baby need not worry because he has his mother to take care of him. Do we have a Father to take care of us? Surely we have and He has commanded us not to worry nor be anxious about our existence. Can we learn? Yes we can and we must learn and live as He has commanded us to; free from all the anxieties that perplexes the world. If our Father has given us the Kingdom then what else will He not give us? Let us try Him for a change; this is my challenge to us all.

We own this truth and no one can pluck it from us. This indeed is our experience now. Once we only heard of Him but now we are experiencing Him in His glory and see Him in His Majesty. We now experience Him as Isaiah did: "High and lifted up." Yet as we see and experience Him in this way, there are others who see Him in the very opposite light. Some see Him as the cruel taskmaster who punishes as soon as one does wrong and who will in the end send them to Hell. They fail to see Him as He is; Full of Grace and Truth. Not willing that any should perish but that all should come to repentance. Some feel quite justified in their hatred of God because He is apart as the absolute Truth and that He is absolutely sovereign. In essence, He has become their rivals as did Satan.

Wouldn't they like to share in the sovereignty of the holy God, so that they could in time become as Lucifer, a usurper? It is only the humble and contrite heart that will see God and share in His splendour and will reign with Him.

15 It is only in this state that we have an interest in Jesus Christ and in the eventful administration of the universe. "If we suffer, we shall also reign with Him:" 2 Timothy 2:12. It is only as submissive partners shall we reign and not as usurpers and unrighteous rivals.

God, the Almighty God, flung the stars and suns and moons into their orbits and they stay in their places and function, each as they should for as long as they are there and their functions are predictable, we set our clocks by them and even our nuclear warheads by them and yet man cannot stay in his place neither does he know his place. He is restless and corrosive and antagonist to his Maker, always crossing the boundaries and plotting his own paradigm. He is forever wondering and doubting as to his position in this universe. The sun which is set in our solar system does not cross over to rival other suns nor vice versa. They rotate in an orderly manner year in and year out for as long as God shall allow them to.

Man on the other hand, in his sinful state is bewildered; he cannot find rest for his wandering soul. He is likened to the stars that Jude speaks of: "… wandering stars, to whom is reserved the blackness of darkness forever." Jude 13. To be in such a position is reprehensible to the sensitive soul, and to the conscience that still functions, the thought of such a place is stifling and suffocating. At the thought of this possibility we Christians must humble ourselves and fall on our knees and pray the prayer of Habakkuk: "O Lord, I have heard thy speech, and was afraid: O Lord, revive thy work in the midst of the years, in the midst of the years make known; in wrath remember mercy." Habakkuk 3:2. If mercy was not one of God's attributes then we would be consumed a long time ago because the world surely is not a friend of God, we are antagonistic toward Him when we remain in our sin.

In summation, the whole duty of man is encapsulated in Ecclesiastes 12:13. "Let us hear the conclusion of the whole matter: Fear God, and keep His commandments: for this is the whole duty of man." At what point will we humans lay down our arms and reconcile a truce with our Maker? Should we wait until we are beaten and cornered with no hope of reconciliation?

God help us to see our condition that we cannot win the battle, it is fixed and we are the losers. Paul states in 2 Corinthians 5:20. "…we pray you in Christ's stead, be ye reconciled to God." We have the pleadings of a man whose brilliance and erudition was reduced to ashes after his encounter with the Risen Saviour, who now bares his heart and soul in in his appeal to us who are still resisting the Holy Spirit and remain disconnected from God's grace.

Give it up John, give it up Mary; the reasonable thing to do is to surrender all to Jesus. As the song writer, Judson W. Van De Venter puts it. "All to Jesus I surrender, all to Him I freely give." This is the only way to go, surrendering all to Him.

16 God is sovereign and His power will never be diminished, a fact we should learn early and surely. Following Christ and delivering the good news is common sense; it is not striving and planning and devising new ways to present the Gospel but simply delivering it with love and sincerity from a heart that is touched itself. The power and effectiveness is the Word itself, the Good News if you will that *"Jesus saves."*

The God I have come to know and embrace has given me a deal and it is pure and simple, unique and immeasurable. It is God condescending in the person of Jesus Christ who came to earth to rescue me. In response, I give Him my love and gratitude from now on and throughout all eternity. As I meditate on the gravity of this reality, I realize that my eternity starts here and now. I have already entered into His eternal rest and I claim or make this claim on the authority of His word. Why should I struggle and experience unrest when this is my standing. I am now in my

Father's house and under His care and all is well. Amen. What can go wrong when He supervises all my goings and comings? Psalm 121:8. This is the vehicle which I have chosen to travel on the road to happiness and it is indestructible. We have only to remain fervent in His service and we are in. No fear no worry. In this respite, we find and hold implicitly. We are no longer restive on our journey from earth to heaven. We are now in good stead by his mercies.

There is a diligence in finding this measure of certainty that cannot be found merely on the surface of our Christianity; we have to be determined miners, digging deep into the recesses of the Scriptures to unravel or to discover the magnificent truths that are contained therein. It took Martin Luther many years to fully absorb a simple passage of Scripture. Romans 1:17. "For therein is the righteousness of God revealed from faith to faith: as it is written, The just shall live by faith." He declared finally when it sank in: "When I discovered that, I was born again of the Holy Ghost. The doors of paradise swung open, and I walked through." It finally dawned on him that the righteousness which was now his was not achieved actively by indulgences but passively by faith alone. That it was *Justitia Alienum* an alien righteousness given by God Himself which is *extra nos and* quite outside of ourselves. The righteousness is a gift which one does not work for. It is given freely with no strings attached. One only has to receive it. Salvation is this gift of God and only has to be received by you and me. It is not obtained in any other way.

Martin Luther declared after he had received his salvation, that if *Monkery* could get one into heaven he would surely be in. He was a Monk and did more than was expected of him as one; so fervent was his passion for the order. Yet he was distressed in his soul. There was no peacein his soul until he discovered the portion of Scripture which speaks of salvation by faith. Romans 1:17. Men everywhere in all religions seek peace with self and with

God but none will be found outside of Christ. He alone is the Author and giver of peace.

17 Religion of our own making does not amount to much. Religion not founded on Scripture is only a form of rituals but one which denies the power of God. It is useless. We must choose this day whom we will serve and as Joshua challenged the Israelites, we too have a choice to make. Neutral we cannot be, we must take one side or the other. When we scrutinize the matter carefully we will discover that we have two basic dimensions. First and foremost we are spiritual beings embodied in an earthly body. The real tangible person is in essence the soul. Our bodies are like an appendage of ourselves. A toe or a hand can be removed and the body still manages and lives on; likewise, a body can be dead and the person lives on. The soul and the real person is indestructible, it does not or cannot die. It is in this dimension that we should make the greatest investment.

Often times I hear my wife using this expression. "My body is not well. "Meaning it will not allow her to do the things she wants to do. The body hinders the person from doing something which that person needs to do. This body is a mighty enhancer of life but it is not the life bearing engine we think it is. This part of us is subjected to decay and ultimately death but the soul lives on, it dwells in another dimension eternally. Herein lays our dilemma when we live outside of Christ. As we live, we move the body around at will; ordering it to do our bidding but what then after that body is gone, is dead, it cannot be ordered anymore. Well first, or then we become a disembodied soul with a destination of one of two places; Heaven or Hell. The time we spent with our bodies was a time when we had the opportunity to consider and decide where we want to spend our eternity. We have the chance and opportunity to prepare for the everlasting dwelling place. Did we make good on deciding where or did we frivolously live our lives without considering such a possibility. At death, reality sets in; no longer does one have the chance to play the fool. One's condition is forever fixed and that soul forever is deprived of any ability to change positions. Does such an outlook shake us a little, or does it awakens us to reality fully?

I am only the messenger delivering the message. *"Look and live."* Beyond this vale or curtain lies a panoramic vista, no eye has ever seen or mind can imagine what lies there and are awaiting the Christians. We only have to strive and persevere to obtain that which is prepared for us. This is the kind of perseverance and striving that Paul speaks of: "Striving toward the mark of the high calling of God in Christ Jesus." Straining and exerting as it were, every fibre to attain the depths of the truths of the Scriptures; this is what is required of us. All of this can be wrapped up into one word. "Growth" We must continue to grow as children and reach maturity eventually so that our possession will be unmistakably ours.

In essence, we are greatly lacking in our faith. It remains essentially underdeveloped and stunted and in history, there are only a few saints throughout the ages who have exhibited

18 Great faith. The rest of us are lacking miserably. No wonder Jesus chided His disciples who witnessed so many miracles and yet at times doubted. He said to them that if they had faith as small as a mustard seed they could move mountains.

We discredit our Maker every day when we worry and doubt His word which was meant for us. There are numerous promises for us and we belittle all or most of them almost as a rule. Our faith is small also and as such we remain unfulfilled and impotent to a great extent. God has made those promises to his children but we still do not grasp the import or significance of them, and as such we live as ordinary citizens. The law of the Spirit who gives life has set us free from the law of sin and death and we continue to live as though we remain in bondage. Freed without realizing it, that is the way most of us live; still attached to the world. We are pegged to it and every time it rolls we must follow.

Even after the *"Emancipation proclamation"* was signed by President Abraham Lincoln on April 16, 1862 which effectively freed all slaves in the United States many remained at their posts not realizing that they were indeed freed. That some did not hear the good news and others did not believe it, while others simply were satisfied to stay on as part of the households in which they worked. Which category does some of us Christians fall in; are we feeling the exhilaration of being set free and enjoying that freedom or is it still of little importance to us. The impartation of Christ's righteousness to us is the best news since creation but is it still just blasé to some of us? We cannot hide the way we feel, we show it by our lives; in our living and in our giving, it is not hidden in any way shape or form, it is out in the open. We are read daily by the world and we must be more careful about the things we write on those pages. May God help us to take stock now and always as we make our way through this life? We are responsible persons, responsible to Go and proclaim the "Good News" and we must also act the part of sobriety and vigilance. We are the salt and the Light of the world.

No longer are we under the law of sin and death which condemns. Sin has no more dominion over us neither is death. Those are relics of the past and are as passé as the flat earth is. Our lives are structured differently now and under God we will prevail over sin, we must prevail over sin and unrighteousness. We are in a new household and a new family now where our commands are to walk circumspectly in a dark world. Our position as children has been procured by the God of Heaven Himself, so what is hindering us from taking our positions at His table? This question I am truthfully asking and asking it that some reader might find an answer for such a question. Why are we not living triumphantly? These are questions that I am looking for answers to for myself also. The ordinary life does not suffice anymore; I am looking for the supernatural intervention on a daily basis. I want to see God at work in the life of His children that would separate us from the mundane life of the unbeliever. Let us band together and ask

19 for such blessings. These are the things I have been trying to express in this book; a message to the believers to be the people we are meant to be and not to belittle our positions.

Let us examine John 3:16. "For God so loved the world that he gave his only begotten Son, that whosoever believeth in Him should not perish, but have everlasting life." Personally I am claiming all that is offered in this verse. I will not perish in the future that is true but today, right now, I have in the present tense *"Everlasting Life."* When I surrendered my life to God, the promise of eternal life rolled over from a promise to a gift. Now that I have my gift, how should I now manage it, how shall I use it, how shall I benefit from it? Simply put, what use is it to me now. That's the question?

The story is told of a man who had a great lump of gold which he used as a door stopper. It was his, he owned it but the value was untapped, he lived an ordinary life with his riches tied up unused. It was of no monetary value to him until it was discovered that it was gold. Likewise, we have our great resource in Christ Jesus and we nevertheless live in poverty. Shame on us I say.

Being in this state, the possessor of the most valuable commodity, if I can call it that, I must rejoice and settle back to enjoy some eternal bliss. You might say I might as well get some practice while I am here and that is exactly what I plan to do for the rest of my life. I am living by faith and my faith will beat the odds; I am living the irrational life, the abnormal and the illogical life. It is living in the supernatural realm because my God is the God of the impossible. I cannot fall back and resign myself to accepting what is normal anymore. Normalcy is for the carnal man. In light of the foregoing statement, I have become a "Martyr" simply dead to the world and its allurements. This is where we all should be as Christians; true believers acting out our faith. Paul states in: Galatians 2:20. "I am crucified with Christ:

nevertheless I live; yet not I, but Christ liveth in me: and the life which I now live in the flesh, I live by the faith of the Son of God, who loved me and gave himself for me." This is a fact whether realized or not, this is the true state of the "Believer." That we are crucified or have been crucified with Christ at Calvary is as real as night follows day. The old person has died and we now live in newness of life with our Risen Lord. This is the state we should be conscious of, living triumphantly over pain and distresses and hardships. Though they present themselves, they must not assail us. We have the remedy for all the maladies. The world must see and know that we have been with Jesus. We must reflect His light as the moon reflects the suns. Embracing the new life, therefore, is dying to the world and living in newness of life by cultivating our faith. Cultivating our faith means we are to give our full attention to keeping it in the forefront and to be attentive in keeping it watered and fed, day in and day out until we

20 close our eyes in death or until Christ returns to take us home. We do this notwithstanding the pain we feel each day, for we must not try to deny the pain in a Stoic manner and pretend that they are not real. Our pain are as real as everybody's else's but as we glow in the anticipatory joy ahead of us we carry our burdens and count our blessings as we move on through life.

The vicissitudes of life will produce character and wisdom from which we will be able to assist others in similar circumstances. Strength is developed through hardships and that is now our forte; "Strength." "Be strong in the Lord and in the power of His might," we are told. Ephesians 6:10. Having put on the whole armour of God, Paul commanded us to be strong. Paul is not making a suggestion here, he is giving a directive and it is in the imperative. This command goes for every living person who names the name of Christ. I would not waste space here to begin to show some of our weaknesses, we all know how pathetic some of our behaviours are.

It is not the calm and placid sea that brings out the sailor's skills but the boisterous storm that pound the ship; that is his test and not a peaceful voyage. The Lord sends us hardships at times I am sure, to test our mettle and to strengthen our fortitude as we move toward the finish line. Many of us will finish as seasoned veterans and we will have reason to rejoice the more for our sufferings. Some of us will have become masters at the art of suffering in the ordinary vicissitudes of life and may never be called or be put upon to suffer for Christ but whichever path our journey takes us, let us be faithful soldiers. Let us show the world that our path is secure, despite the hindrances and setbacks that we face. When the war is over and the soldiers start the homeward march, that is a scene to behold, it is like no other. The march consists of only survivors be it some with no hands, one leg or bandaged unrecognisable; they hold and aid each other with a unity not seen at any other time during the campaign. The bright eyes and smiles signifies something glorious, it signifies hope; ahead is home and hope regardless of their present conditions. They are heading home as survivors and overcomers and that is a wonderful feeling. Many times however, that hope is stifled and ruined by circumstances we know that to be true. Unlike the soldiers however, the Christians however, maimed, will be marching into a glorious new life where disappointments is not rear, it is nonexistent. No more tears, no more heartaches nor headaches, our victory over live will have been complete and the doors to our glorious rest opened. This is hope personified; nothing more need be added.

Act now dear brother, dear sister and do not wait to be "floativated." The ability to endure hardships lie deep within each of us; in other words, it is even at hand so to speak and we must live within its parameters to reap the full blessings and reach our greatest potential. God has promised to be with us whatever betides. We as the redeemed can now sing; "Great is thy faithfulness." Let us shine that spiritual light with its many beams of colour which

21 Encompasses; knowledge, joy, holiness and exuberance, into a dark world, a world that lacks any semblance of stability and reality; a world that is building on the shifting sands of time.

We must begin to live as possessors of eternal life and dwellers in this glorious hope that encompasses our new status as prince and princesses and not continue as paupers and beggars. We belong to the Kingdom of God and heirs of His promises, therefore, our lives must show it. We must triumph over evil, all day and every day. We must purge evil from our thoughts and our actions completely, even from our systems as though we were taking a cleansing agent so that we can live as children of Light. We have new hearts and a new destiny. Fruit bearing is only a matter of abiding in the vine. As long as we keep connected, we will inevitably bear fruit. Fruit bearing is a must; it is a natural outcome of being in the vine. In light of this glorious prospect, how can we ever be discouraged? How can we fail to sing His praises when He provides our security, provision and our peace?

Distraction is a ploy or a tool the evil one uses to get us off course at times. He has his devices but we must never forget that the battle is fixed. We are already victorious and there is nothing to fear. It is not a hit or miss proposition, we are victors and God help us to realize that fact and help us to live as though we are indeed victors. I see it all around me, in churches and on the streets, Christian card carrying members acting as pathetic beings. Some will not refrain from gossiping, others will not relinquish the bottle and so on and these are only what we see publicly. How sobering it is when you meet someone and enquire about a brother or a sister who ran into trouble and hear them say we cannot discuss what happened. We are not allowed to talk about it. They simply will not prolong the agony. How honourable that is dear friends. Some people have truly learned the art of discretion and have the tongue securely under control. I say kudos to such a brother or a sister.

Since we have this hope, this confident expectation that we will rise again (*Resurgam*) even if we die before He comes again, then why should not we rise above every vile circumstance and mount up as eagles. *"Ad astra per aspera."* (To the stars through difficulties) We reign supreme now over sin and circumstances. Difficulties and sin working against us are but instruments on which we can hone our craft. We are called to be overcomers and if there were not difficulties and problems then what would we overcome? The darker the night the brighter the light shines. Personally, I am confident that all my difficulties will be surmounted, the problems solved and duty will be done in the end. Then I will see in hindsight that life was not a burden or a problem to be solved but an adventure to be experienced. I am now seeing all of this in the rear view mirror as I journey home.

22 We are builders, all of us; those in Christ and those outside of Christ; albeit each side builds different buildings and each hope to have a different outcome. We all for the exception of a few were building on the opposite side and know now that our buildings would not stand the fiery trials. Now we build on a sure foundation and invite the Master builder to be our Architect. We give Him full reign in our enterprise and know confidently that He is able to aid us in its completion. As such, we can invoke the three Ws. We don't worry, we do not waver and we do not weaken. We can stay upright and erect, for we are overcomers. The question is; are we pursuing, are we finding and are we holding?

God has given us everything to fortify our lives against sin. He has given us His Holy Spirit to indwell us and in Him we are complete. Let us then, therefore, personalize and actualize this prodigious event that Christ in us is the hope of Glory. Considering now our fortification, we are more than conquerors through Him that loved us. We must dare walk in the light of

His redemptive and overcoming work of Calvary. "It is finished" Christ said on the Cross and here we have it. We can now walk in that freedom, not doubting, not wavering, only enjoying. He has given us everything pertaining to godliness. 2 Peter 1:3: While the world is running on empty, seeking after earthly endeavours and possessions, we the Christians are walking confidently and securely, not stumbling nor fainting. We have an advocate with our Father in times of difficulty anytime, anywhere, day or night. We have an open line through prayer to the portals of heaven to the King of Kings and one cannot begin to imagine how satisfying that is when such a statement is personalized. The transaction has been accomplished, the Devil is a defeated foe and we are free citizens.

At timDiswe might be one seemingly lonely person, walking or driving on our own, doing our uttermost to keep our sanity but we must never forget that even then we are not alone. This temporary existence calls for fortitude in such times, for it will not be long before we are taken or called home and then it will be joy unspeakable. In light of such a glorious future let us bear our burdens with a smile. We know what's in store for us and as such we can exercise patience in all that we do. The anxious moments are experiences of the past; we now live in peace with self and God and with earnest expectation of a good end. Let us then pursue this new lifestyle with gusto and ride the waves relishing every moment we are given.

CHAPTER 3

CHRIST THE ANCHOR OF OUR SOULS

23 If Christ be not the anchor of our souls, then we flounder and are tossed like a ship without a rudder upon the high seas.

As I view things daily and assess the present situation around me, I wonder what I would be like not having an anchor for my soul. Just living without any real purpose? Hippocrates, the father of medicine states: *"There are, in effect, two things: To know and to believe one Knows."* In essence, this is what this book is all about. It is to bring us closer to the truth. It is to spur us on to know and to encourage us to plumb the depths of the Scriptures and to know that we do know. Not living by heresy but on facts.

We can now confidently as believers say; I know that Jesus died for me and that He is now living in me and directing my life. That we have passed the stage of believing and have entered the stage of knowing and experiencing, we no longer believe in God but we know Him intimately. This is the message I wish this book will convey to its readers.

As I speak to so called Christians I hear a doubt expressed frequently at the direct question. "Are you saved?" The reply invariably will be. "I hope so." Are we jokers or what We are partakers of something and we are not sure what it entails or teaches. It begs the question as to whether we are serious or even curious about what we believe. If I ask the same person, if he is married; he will be sure to give an answer. He will give me a yes or no answer without hesitation. Why, because he is dealing with a factual event and not an imaginary one; he is not living in an illusionary dimension.

In his Poem, *"A Psalm of Life"* Henry Wadsworth Longfellow states:

> Tell me not in mournful numbers,
> Life is but an empty dream,
> For the soul is dead that slumbers,
> And things are not what they seem.
> Life is real! Life is earnest!

Some of us ought to pinch ourselves sometimes to verify the fact that we are indeed alive and are still living in a real world. Of course, life is real and life is earnest and we must live it earnestly and realistically so that a good outcome will be the result. Our existence is a real one a substantive one. Although at times we wish things were otherwise, yet we know it is not so. Things will not just disappear, they are here to stay.

24 In His New Testament or His will, our names are written there and the official seal is imprinted on that document which makes it as authentic as any document gets. It is not hard for you to know if your name is in that book. You will know as you read this book whether you have trusted Him for your salvation or you are still putting your trust in man's vain philosophy. In my circle of information, every day I read where men and women of all ages and from all religions trust the Lord Jesus Christ in whom there is life and enjoyment. Just today I read this man's testimony where he said he was deceived for forty years. He grew up in a church and would have died and gone to Hell if he had not received through radio the message of the Gospel. You who are reading this sentence right now do not play the fool. Make your calling

an election sure. In 2 Peter 1:10 we are admonished: "wherefore the rather, brethren, give diligence to make your calling and election sure: for if ye do these things, ye shall never fall"

This portion of scripture is quite suggestive I believe. It is encouraging us to hold fast as it were, for a lot is riding on us. If we do these things we shall never fall is placing the onus on us the believers. We would better work out our own salvation as it were.

James too was not wasting words when he declared this fact that we cannot go about spouting faith, faith and faith alone. He emphasized the fact when he says here: "Even so faith, if it hath not works, is dead, being alone. Yea, a man may say, Thou hast faith, and I have works: show me thy faith without thy works, and I will show thee my faith by my works" James 2:17. A father might never tell his kids that he loves them, he might never hugged nor kissed them but he labours to provide for them and he is home as often as he can to protect them at nights, therein expressing his love for them. Our faith is expressed in the same manner to our father when we labour in his vineyard in whatever way we can to enlarge His kingdom. It is by our works that they shall know that we are Christ's. (We are not to confuse works as a means to salvation, for it is not; we can only work after we are saved).

It is in Christ that all our hopes and expectations lie. Through Him and in Him alone we are absolved from our sins and have access to eternal life. Christ is our all in all. He is all we need to enter into our rest. He is in effect our rest but we must enter. We must take the initiative to enter or to admit Him into our lives. There are many falsehood out there, many dead religions vying for our souls; we must do our due diligence to seek and to find the one which is able to transform our lives and to secure our future. Christ Jesus is indeed the real deal, everything else is falsehood. He is your only guarantee for a secure future.

Remember the phrase: "El mundo parace pequeno" The opinion of the world is small. The world might make a loud and boisterous cry but it is never right about eternal matters. It is in

25 the quiet region of your heart that eternal matters are sorted out and settled. The Holy Spirit will be bearing witness with your spirit that you are His if you have trusted in Him. Many are crying: "You must have Jesus." and are themselves bowing down to idols, the hypocrisy is palpable. You owe it to yourself to check things out, make sure what you are promised is what you will get. If what you are promised cannot be verified by God's word then it is suspect. If it is not stated in the Bible, then we are on the wrong track. When you can fill in the blank with your own name then you can rejoice but until then keep on seeking.

Where the Scriptures declare: "Come unto me and I will give you rest for your soul." If you can fill in your name after: Come unto me … and I will give you rest" then you are in. You have entered the great plan of Salvation which the Lord drew up before the foundation of the world. If you have reached this point of consciousness in your life and have taken this step, then you will have fulfilled your mission in life by enlisting in the service of the Master.

In my book "*What's Up?*" I told some of my school bus students that I was writing a book and they all wanted their names in it. I told them that I would make mention of them as a group but that each name could not be in it, however I saw where because of a certain incident that I could use a name and I asked permission from that young man to use his name. Well, you can imagine how excited he was and of course, wants a copy of the book as soon as it gets published. It is ready as I write this sentence and I am to deliver it to him shortly. Just to see his name in print and for many of us the first time we saw our names on a card or in print we too were excited. If such trivial matters can delight us, how much more when we know our names are written in the Lambs Book of Life in Heaven. Is your name .... written there?

To have that assurance is peace personified and joy unspeakable. Trevor Turner's name is in that book. Living with this reality makes every yesterday a dream of happiness and every tomorrow a vision of hope for me. Life has reached its zenith when one is in Christ and that is without adoubt.

We now stand between two realities

In eons past we stood with our father Adam in the beautiful Garden of Eden and we fellowshipped with God and enjoyed his fatherly love and companionship and something happened to change His attitude toward us. Our father Adam disobeyed God and as a consequence we inherited the curse that was pronounced upon mankind because of his disobedience. The human race from then on was destined to a life of suffering and dying. No 26 longer would man live forever in a blissful surrounding. Even the earth on which he lived was then cursed and subjected to briars and thorns, yielding a meagre subsistence. Hardship from then on was the way of life; this became our inescapable destiny. We became a people who had to till the soil to survive and from then on our indulgencies became varied and sometimes even prodigious. We grew into a people who wanted to behave like Cain; stubborn and rebellious against our Maker. In essence we became and remain restless and haunted, always seeking after the illusionary dream.

This condition was not to remain fixed and unchangeable however; God promised to send us His son who would die on the Cross to secure our rightful place again with Him. God the Father promised this rebellious and wondering people a Redeemer. That was fulfilled over two thousand years ago and since then; men and women everywhere have renewed their relationship with their Maker. Men and women have been revelling in the joy of sins forgiven and have been dying with a smile on their faces as they anticipate their entrances into God's glorious presence. Now in Christ Jesus our relationship with God has been restored and we can again call Him father. We are a family again. Thank God for the Redeemer, Jesus Christ His son.

Those of us who have been separated from our families for whatever reason and have been restored or reunited, know what it is to belong again. The home coming is marvelous and exhilarating to say the least. Restoration and fellowship is one of our greatest blessings as human beings. Many a father or a mother wonder and are deeply saddened over the loss or waywardness of a child and are hurting continually until that one returns and the fellowship is restored. Many of us likewise are in that position right now and until we return to the Father He will be dishearten. Christ cried over Jerusalem when he saw the wonderings of His people and their rebellion against Him.

In spite of our rebellion however, God is working diligently in the midst of our confusion and as such there is a big, BUT as in Adam we all die, now in Christ we are made alive when we believe in Him. Christ is our new Adam in Life. This is wondrous Grace, marvelous and true and the sooner it sinks in the better off we will be. We are now made alive in Christ. The body is susceptible to disease and eventual death but the soul is eternal and lives on. Jesus Christ expounded upon this fact when in Mathew 10:28 He states: "And fear not them which kill the body, but are not able to kill the soul…" Now we have an everlasting soul which will be reunited to a new body after death in the second coming of Christ.

The fact is that, ourselves will not be buried with our remains, but ourselves will remain or live on eternally in one place or another. Seneca, Galileo's brother, philosopher and tutor to Nero said: *"The body is the prison of the soul and death is praised as release, as the birthday of*

27 *eternity."* If such a statement rings true to us as Christians, should not we then be excited to depart this dreary confused world? I am getting anxious to make my departure to be truthful. Even as Christians, we fight for a few more days here on earth when we become ill and harass our dying bodies for what? If we are moving on to a better place, why fight then for a few more months or a year here? I can't see it. As for me, I live in readiness

so that when death knocks, I am not begging for more time. I want to respond with a smile on my face.

The Apostle Paul in Philippians 1.21 says: "For to me to live is Christ, and to die is gain." Paul here is unveiling or unmasking his soul, his heart and his very being. Everything is summed up in this one sentence. His life is not worldly, engrossed with the baggage of this life. He is a free man and he is ready to depart this temporary abode for his expansive eternal dwelling place. How comforting it is to know that our new home after conversion is not dreary and haphazard and cruel and damaging in any way to our existence but pure and beautiful and splendid. The thought is stupendous. The reality will be out of this world indeed.

I often hear touching testimonies of miracles in one's life which encourages us to press on but why should we be alarmed when there are miracles. This is the sphere in which we should be living. We should live in a state of unnatural events as the norm, where our Father takes care of us as we would our own children. If we analyze the situation carefully we would come to the conclusion that the Lord cares and gives us what we need abundantly. Matthew 7:9-11 Jesus said: "Or what man is there of you, who if his son asks bread, will give him a stone. 11 If ye then, being evil, know how to give good gifts unto your children, how much more shall your father which is in heaven give good things to them that ask Him?" As we meditate on this statement by Christ, we must confess that we are not living by the faith of the Lord Jesus Christ who loved us and gave himself for us and even at this juncture we can stop and say a prayer. "Lord Jesus, increase my faith to believe you totally; not partially: Amen."

In the space of four or five years I have counted six miracles on the road; incidences and accidents which the Lord had saved me from. I recount some of them occasionally but not frequently because I have come to realize that my life in God's hand is a life of supernatural interventions. I take care as best I can but when the difficulties arise He is there to deal with it. He and not I is able to handle all the hardships and it is His pleasure to do so, so why not allow Him to do as He sees fit. Since God is able I should no longer be using the conditional clause "If" and from now on I will substitute if for "Since." Now since God is able and we believe He is, then why not simply hand over the reins of our lives to Him completely. Allow Him to handle our affairs.

28 At a prayer meeting a brother wanted me to give these or at least some of them as a testimony but I said we should not be living in the past, but rather be experiencing Him now, every day in the present. Here is where I want to live, in the present. The Lord might have been the God of Jacob, Abraham and Isaac but He is my God now also. I want to experience His power as they did.

We do not always ask for the blessings we receive because it is already the Father's good pleasure to shower us with them and furthermore, the Lord Jesus Christ has made it His duty to pray for us constantly. I believe too that at other times we keep crying out for what we are already in possession of. Like the greedy child who cries out for more and more when they have enough to keep them happy and occupied. In spite of our prodigious supply as children of God, we still cry for more and more and just when will we be comforted by this world's goods; for some of us, never? We continue to sing the world's sad song when we should have forgotten it light years ago and adopt a new song that lightens our steps and brightens our paths.

Truly, we are complete in Christ and there is nothing more to be added; of course, some of us are missing it miserably when we fail to live out our new life in its fullness. It is subsistence living when we fail to live in light of the wondrous word and precious promises of God. We know it, we feel it and we desire better but we will not invest as much as we must in the kingdom. We must have mastery over this life and to do so we can only prepare to spend more time with the Master. More time with Him means delving in His word and in prayer. Many of us should get to know

Him well by now. Some of us have been walking with Him for many, many, years and yet our conversation belies that walk. We remain strangers and foreigners as though we do not belong to His household.

Have you ever known a child who doesn't want to come into the house at night? No, never. He comes home where he feels safe. He draws near to his home as night falls and gets insidewhere he belongs. God has given us that capacity for fellowship and we are not ourselves until we enjoy that close fellowship with each other but especially with Him.

The fellowship we enjoy with our Father brings us into His great blessings. He is now our shepherd and as such we shall not want. Our wants or needs are met in Him especially our greatest need which is forgiveness. The need to be set free from our sin and guilt and burden of sin is indeed our greatest need. There is no greater freedom than to be freed of those debilitating vices. Now that we have that burden like Paul Bunyan rolled away, we can move forward with ease to the promise land. This realization should hasten our steps and broaden our smile indeed.

29 We move now lightly not just as overcomers but as conquerors. We are part of a marching army which is formidable; nothing or no one can thwart our progress. We are a mighty force with Christ as our commander in chief. With Him we are invincible and we must believe it. In Romans 8:37 Paul states: *"Nay, in all these things we are more than conquerors through Him that loved us."* Now this assurance should strengthen our determination in the fight. To have this assurance is to know that we cannot fail in our march toward the finish line. The battle is fixed and the enemy is defeated, he is vanquished. He knows it himself but many of us do not know it yet.

How much clearer must our paths be mapped out? We now only need to open our understanding and see that the engagement we are in is real and we are marching unto Zion and there is no power on earth that can keep us down. We reign supreme. In

Christianity, there is no ambiguity; everything is made crystal clear to the person who desires to know. I trust that God will give us all the desire to know Him and to know Him intimately where we will have the confidence that when we ask, He will answer us. We must keep on revising and entertaining our minds least things slip away especially as we grow older. We have to live in the Word of God to remain relevant. We must ever be mindful that the enemy and his *Modus Operandi* will devise ways to remove us from the Truths of God's word. We will have to be diligent students of the Word, never ever letting up. We should never relent in the search of God's word for treasure and favours. We are already in His favour when we acknowledge Him as Saviour and Lord, so to ask for what we need and even desire are His pleasure to give. By now the timidity should be gone and confidence reign instead in our approach to the Lord. He declares that we can come boldly to Him so why don't we?

Moses and King Hezekiah are men who pleaded with God for what we would call favours and God granted them their requests. He listened to them then, why not us now also. Faith for these men did not come overnight; they practiced their faith over time and as someone has said: *"Faith is growth into God — leaning into Him."* The Bible labels men of great faith as ordinary men, like you and me. They had no greater credentials than us but their faith became their credentials after the facts. God is open to our cries today as in the days that He was on earth. There is no difference and we wonder why there are so few miracles today in our lives. Is it because we have other things to trust in, why we have not trusted Him as we ought? When I was at West Toronto Baptist Church there was a dear brother who told us that he had a rich brother whom he witnessed to all the time and the brother would reply. "Clair, you have your God and I have my money. When I need some money I go to the bank and you, you go to your God." In this case one brother's god has become his money.

Then we will ask; how each is faring now in his separate abode? Since both have already departed this life.

30 The state of Israel spends a disproportionate amount of their GDP on armaments because of course; their trust is now in their armaments and not God. A whopping half of their GDP is spent on arms to defend themselves against their enemies, whereas in times past when they knew their God, He was their defence. Let us as Christians learn to trust our God for all that is necessary for our survival. Let us trust Him for our future security and never worry about not having enough for instance, when retirement comes. Everything and not somethings are in His hands and we are His most prized possessions, so then we are indeed secure in His care.

Each of us must search and find our shortcomings and repent and come clean before God. He delights in truthfulness and that is why He warns us that our sins will find us out. Confess your sins before or to God and allow Him to forgive you and start with a clean slate. Do not wait for a catastrophe, and then you confess. God will be pleased that you come to Him in confession and repentance. As a matter fact, He is waiting with outstretched arms for your return.

At the new birth we have this confident knowledge that we are now the children of God and as such we have new life. We have already been raised to newness of life from death in our trespasses and sins. Since the most that can be expected is already ours, why should we doubt that other things would be a problem for our Father to give us? This is our new reality that we are forgiven and that Christ and not Adam is ordering and directing our future. God be praised. Since our souls are anchored in Christ, what then shall we fear and what more can we hope for. We are now complete In Him, glory to God. Colossians 2:10.

CHAPTER 4

THE REVISIONIST'S DILEMMA

The revisionists come on the scene with their brilliance and try to play little gods. They set themselves up and proceed to tell us that things are not what we make them out to be. They say that they can prove to us that the idea of God and creation is a myth. The doctrine of God and creation which we hold dear is only a figment of our imaginations and such things are not for the intelligencia of which they are a part.

They have discovered from their intellect and study and by observation that the animals have evolved from nothing into what we see today. God definitely has nothing to do with what we call creation. These are they who have been sent by the gods to enlighten us and to open our eyes to the real world. They say Christians falsify the records and we deceive the nations.

31 Beware of them. However, since they come as bearers of lofty letters they must be right, so they have a large following. I must reiterate, be aware of these false prophets on the scene, sometimes they come as angels of light but they are wolves in sheep's clothing. They are working for Satan the Devil and do not know it. Their portion will be with Him in the lake of fire. Please do not keep company with such either, they are pernicious beasts. Close examination is required before the full extent of the damage

of their devious ways can be assessed. The damage is being done as they sway the minds of the vulnerable. These are sophists coming with the express purpose to deceive and to corrupt.

We hear much about relativism and reductionism in the market place these days. Everything that is set forth now is relative; it is what you make of it, what you think of it. There are no absolutes; things are always changing and the truth lies in the interpretation we are made to understand but for you the reader I want to be absolute with you. The reason I want to be absolute with you is that you are reading, therefore you are searching and developing. You have not remained static in your condition like so many, waiting for all things to happen, nor have you remained dormant or impotent about what is happening. You are not allowing things to wash over you like a great tsunami but you are relevant, checking and analysing things for yourself. You have a role to play in your life and the sooner you realize it, the better it is for you. You have already developed into an intelligent person, now you must add wisdom to your knowledge. Wisdom is crossing over the threshold from head knowledge to the heart. You can now see beyond the pragmatic into the spirit world. No longer do you believe that things will disappear into thin air but that each of us is responsible to our Maker.

We spoke of the revisionist who purports to know more than God himself and that is the way some of them portray themselves, notwithstanding only implicitly. A person who makes statements outside of God's word is a reprobate and a liar, seeking to destroy and corrupt others. Roman Catholic scholar and author Raymond Panikkar, argues in his book: *The Unknown Christ of Hinduism* that Hindus worship the same God as Christians and that God mediates salvation to them through Christ though Christ is unknown to them. When God changed His *modus operandi* and if he did, why it was not written so we all could be informed about the change. Is He working behind the scenes with some and not all? Has he become a God we cannot trust? These are questions

I would like answered but I am not waiting for an answer, I am taking it upon myself to denigrate this writer as false and an intruder and not a believer. How dare he say God mediates salvation even though Christ is not known to a people?

Let's consider for a moment, two things which amounts to the same thing, though they are very opposites. Could we truthfully say the God we worship as Christians is the same God the Jews worship even though they reject Christ? If we answer in the affirmative then we can

32 accept the version or view that the Hindu God is the same as our God although they do not know Christ. Therefore, to know and reject and not to know, amounts to the same thing as far as I see. No Jew although they are even called God's people will ever enter heaven without coming to Christ first. They cannot reject Him and ever hope to see that place and likewise no Hindu will ever enter either, without first coming to Christ. This is the teaching of my Bible that salvation is in no other but Christ, my Lord and Saviour Jesus Christ. If sincerity is carried out here to its logical conclusion then all religions would have a place in bringing men and women into heaven. No one can put up a sign: *to the unknown God* and hope to be covered by the God of the Bible.

Gunapala Dharmasiri, a Buddhist writer, begins his critique of the Christian concept of God with the words, "The Buddhist did not accept the existence of God. The learned Buddhist monk Narada Maha Thera says: "There are no petitionary or intercessory prayers in Buddhism... The Budda does not and cannot grant earthly favours to those who pray to him. A Buddhist should not pray to be saved, but should rely on himself and strive with diligence to win freedom and win purity." The concept here is that no one can save you, you have committed the sin and you must purify yourself in the end. In essence, self is lord of self, pure and simple according to their doctrine.

A drowning person cannot save themselves; they must get outside help to be saved. If a religion denies the existence of God, then why worry about purifying himself in the end. Since they are not answerable to anyone; they are gods, then all is well. A religious people builds temples or mosques or whatever and worships, they know not whom or what and have no goal in the direction of that worship. Self-actualization is a marvelous thing in that it posits that one is already god and all is well thereafter. The postmodern person is a marvelous being indeed; their achievements are outlandish and they stand in need of little or nothing. They are their own masters and if they were tied to any god previously they have now cut themselves free from such encumbrances. They are now free in theory but not indeed.

Such is now the makeup of our world. We hear even in some prayers that we (the Christians) should not be judgemental; in other words, just let things be. Let everything play out and all will be well. Do not rock the boat. Jesus came and said His religion will pit mother against children and cause a division among even a close knit family, how dare some say do not be judgemental while many are falling headlong into hell because of pernicious teachings. Why were the apostles in so much hot water because they refused to compromise, they were compelled to declare the truth, notwithstanding threats and imprisonment and even death. I would to God that we had the same conviction as they. If Christ has set us a pattern and a standard, let us follow it. When it was necessary He, (Jesus Christ) whipped the abusers of the Lords house, He

33 was angry with the abuse that was brought to the Synagogue. I believe God is angry with some of us also who haven't got the nerve to say what is right and condemn what is wrong. To love is not to upset the *status quo that* is being manly and walking in love. There are too many spineless Christians walking around embracing ecumenism. Was Paul judgemental when he withstood Peter to His face over doctrine? "But when I saw that they walked not uprightly according to the truth of the Gospel..." One cannot gloss over error and let it pass for doctrine when it comes to one's

eternal soul. We must let the truth be known regardless of the outcome.

Matthew 10:35 declares: Jesus speaking: "For I am come to set a man at variance against his father, and the daughter against her mother,…" You simply cannot have your cake and eat it also, you will have to decide what it is you want to do. Hold on to your religion or jump ship and find refuge in the only craft available to save you and that is Jesus Christ. Was Christ's death a frivolous event, or was it an event like no other in order that we might be given the chance to escape Hell; that dreaded place. I can only try to express the agony that Christ felt facing Golgotha but I cannot comprehend it even slightly. Going by the account of the Bible as He contemplated that dreadful cross, I know that it was beyond anything we can imagine or relate to.

This is Jesus' condition when our sins weighted down upon Him. "And being in agony He prayed more earnestly: and His sweat was as it were great drops of blood falling down to the ground." Mathew 22:44. Can we try to enter into His suffering here as the Bible described His condition just before the Cross? This is the extent of Christ's suffering and some belittle such suffering and say God mediates salvation some other way. How will they escape when they themselves have not tasted Salvation? It is tragic that such people would get away with such blatant lies. They try to show themselves learned but fools they are.

Look and actuate your world with the divine imperative. God is calling you to repentance and you will answer Him with a yes or a no. You will at the judgement again answer a question. "What have you done with my son?" No one is going to answer that for you; neither your mother; your father, your teacher, nor any wise guy but yourself. You are responsible for your soul and I urge you to guard it against every falsehood. God has spoken and made provision through His son. You must be born again. John 3:5.

I spoke to a man recently as we waited for our cars to be repaired at the garage and he said he was a Christian too like me but he confessed that he does not read. Reading is a must for our development and I encouraged him to start reading the Bible on a daily basis. There are things we spoke about that he did not know even existed in the Bible. I trust he will take my council. 34 We are geniuses on everything but God's word and as such we fall easily for the Devil's lies. More than anything else, this book is intended to encourage you the reader to become a more diligent person by giving yourself more to the things of God starting by knowing His word. Add reading a portion of Scripture to your daily routine but do not stop either until the day you die. When you cannot see to read anymore, ask your kids or grandkids to read to you. Learn to walk by the Word and you will not stumble.

Whatever your age, if you can read these words and understand them you are responsible to God for whatever you are now doing. I Trevor Turner the author would like to tell you that these words were placed here with a burden; a burden for you the reader and indeed the whole world. I cannot reach the whole world but I am reaching someone like yourself and I am pleading with you to listen and heed these words. 1 Peter 4:7 reads: *"But the end of all things is at hand: be ye therefore sober, and watch unto prayer."* Peter wrote these words many centuries ago and if the end was close then, how much closer is it today. It is good to know when we are close, especially if a precipitous or calamitous event is going to take place so that we can avoid it if possible or prepare for it. We do not want to go on blindly and face it unexpectedly and be overtaken or consumed by such an event without some warning. A sign post perhaps, showing how close we are getting to the calamitous event. No one would not welcome or appreciate some warning in the event of danger ahead. One would be a fool not to welcome such warnings. God is setting before you through these pages such a warning please heed it. The time is short and that is evident in the signs of the times.

Two Priests, who lived close to a bridge that was closed, held out a sign which reads; "Stop! turn around" and a motorist derided them for not minding their own business, and for forcing their religion on them. Shortly after this motorist passed and made his accusation, there was a crash and one Priest said to the other, this is the third one who has crashed since morning, may be the sign should read: "Bridge closed." The Christian is being shunned daily and relegated to nothingness for introducing someone to the Gospel and for trying to turn them around in their headlong journey into Hell. The media suggests boldly that things would be better off without us and so on but little do they know. When we are gone in truth, their existence will be living Hell as you hear them say frequently at some catastrophe.

Looking out for yourself is of paramount importance, for you are answerable to God. You are an existentialist and have been given a will to pursue your destiny. You alone have the right to determine the way you take, be it the high way or the low. After you have left the dependency and guidance of your parents you are on your own. You will not be able to tell God that you wanted to honour your parents by keeping their religion. Do not continue the tradition if you have seen that it leads nowhere. Do not be an addict if they were themselves

35 addicts; take the new path that leads to life everlasting. Find the truth and make it your own, find it and internalize it. Find it and live and die by it. Start living like a somebody, a real person and not a fictitious one where you are neither here nor there; neither hot nor cold. Take a hold of yourself in earnest and begin to live with a real identity.

Coleridge has said: "Happiness can be built only on virtue and must, of necessity have truth as its foundation." Truths are absolutes, they are laws, they are formulae, and they cannot be changed to bear results. Our world srevolves on laws and there is nothing we can do but to live by them if indeed we want to achieve happiness as Coleridge stated. Truth is like the anvil on which all hammers of discordance are crushed. Truth stands like the rock of Gibraltar and as a testimony to the greatness of our

Maker. There is none like our God, His truth endureth forever. Do not wait until it is too late to verify that claim, acknowledge Him now and learn to live with eternity in your physic. If you have never heard His word you have the heavens declaring His glory and the firmament shows His handy work daily. Open your eyes and behold His magnificence.

In our day with all the sophisticated gadgetry, we can predict and forecast great natural events long before they overtake us and as such we are given time to flee to safe refuge. In spite of such warnings we find men and women still stubbornly refusing to budge when the authorities warn them to flee. They remain with one motive; they do not want to depart from their possessions. They would rather go down with it or be consumed with it. Unless we find an escape route we will all perish, we are not getting out alive. The storm clouds are gathering and there is coming a tsunami the world has not experienced since the beginning of time and our only refuge is in Jesus Christ. You can refer to this line as fear mongering but I know it and I am not the only one warning of the impending danger. Give yourself a good distance between this danger and home before it hits. Start moving out now. Take your refuge in Jesus Christ. If you don't, these are words you will hear ringing in your ears for all eternity.

In the Old Testament when God wanted to destroy Sodom and Gomorrah because of their sinfulness He sent an angel to warn righteous Lot to flee. Lot took the warning mildly and would have been consumed himself except that God sent an angel to physically drag him and his family out. Lot had no idea that God's judgement upon Sodom and Gomorrah was imminent until the angel of the Lord came and dragged them out. Even among the rottenness of life we can be grieved but are not willing to take the necessary steps to avoid the evil. We live in a sinful world and we must transcend the sinfulness that surrounds us as Christians. We must accept the fact that all will be consumed one day and that day might be sooner than we think. I hope we can all see it clearly as Christians and not as Lot saw it just vaguely.

36 We cannot linger in the congregation of the dead and expect to do well. We must by God's grace break loose and separate ourselves permanently from this cosmos which seeks to suck us in like a magnet, or as stars are sucked into the black hole.

Our world has entered a realm of eminent extinction; we are in a phase of our existence where nations have the ability to disintegrate and incinerate the entire planet making it barren for millennium to come. I believe without a doubt that that time is upon us. A time when the fullness of our inequity has reached up to God and He has said it is enough. The cup of our wickedness is now full and He must act. 11 Peter 3:10 warns us thus: *"But the day of the Lord will come as a thief in the night; in the which the heavens shall pass away with a great noise, and the elements shall melt with fervent heat, the earth also and the works that are therein shall be burned up."* How very sobering is such a prediction even to the Christians; undisturbed because we have taken refuge in Christ. Is every part of ourselves inside the Rock or is there some part still exposed? You make that determination dear reader.

Men can frame this world as one of grandeur, magnificence and order, philosophising and be enamored in self-aggrandisement, portraying it as one with a great future, where we go from strength to strength and by all likelihood if there was not a prediction to the contrary we would think that. We have come a long way in a short time and while we have conquered and eradicated a lot of diseases and so on we invent machines to do our work and we are masters of our destiny we think. Nevertheless, all this acceleration and brilliance comes or creates anoverlapping between good and evil, right and wrong. There is no longer a right and a wrong way of seeing things. The distinction or line of demarcation is now blurred and in some places totally obliterated. We walk blindly now as in the dark and are stumbling along to oblivion.

Saint Augustine has said: "*The rebellious humans themselves in their sin dominated by the very lust for things which they create have become slaves and not masters.*" The things we have created to serve us have now become our masters and we pant after them with a hunger that cannot be satisfied. The hunger and thirst are insatiable and our creations are now our masters. That is pitiable and disturbing to say the least. Great minds have become only slaves by their own choosing albeit unconsciously. Our egotism and self-centeredness have precipitated our demise. We cannot bear to follow the leading of our Creator, for we want to be free even if it means falling headlong into the abyss.

We often forget that we are pilgrims and strangers here on earth and are here for only a short time; yet we hurry and worry and horde and idolize instead of smelling the roses and enjoy and utilize. Psalm 90: 9 & 12 is a sobering passage of Scripture for us to read often. This portion has an ominous ring to it; it reads: "For all our days are passed away in thy wrath: we

37 spend our years as a tale that is told. 12. So teach us to number our days, that we may apply our hearts unto wisdom." Wisdom is that sixth sense which continues to nudge us back on to the right path after we tend to get off it. It is our GPS if you will that will set us straight again after wondering off course. Wisdom is the application of knowledge. Without wisdom all the knowledge is wasted. It would be like getting heavy rain and having no container to catch even a drop of that water. That abundant rainfall is gone and there is nothing to show for it.

Every now and then we need to be reminded of such passages of Scriptures which bring us in line with reality, lest we forget. We are prone to wonder and we often forget that this world is but a temporary abode. As Christians, we live and work and occupy but we must hold lightly to these things or else we too will be sucked in like the rest of the world. We must live wisely.

We invent cameras to peer into the minutest cells and tissue and send telescopes into the outer reaches of the galaxies trying to see if life exist elsewhere in the universe and when we contact any alien life then we can determine where we came from. It is an illusionary voyage men take periodically to transcend their mundane life here on earth and in the end they become great discoverers of new planets, new moons and so on but fail to reconcile with themselves. The greatest discovery is yet to be made and that is to know oneself; be in control of oneself and be at peace with that self.

Isaiah 26: 3: gives us an effective prescription guaranteed to bring relief from all anxieties and concerns, it reads: *"Thou wilt keep him in perfect peace, whose mind is stayed on thee: because he trusteth in thee."* This verse coupled with that of Philippians 4:7. *"And the peace of God which passeth all understanding, shall keep your hearts and minds through Christ Jesus."* Both portions of Scripture deal with the most elusive of all longings and that is peace. The heart that is stayed upon Jehovah will be fully blessed and will find as He promised perfect peace and rest. This position is the greatest state a person can find himself in; the mind at peace with God and self.

This peace of God is a restoration to normalcy. It is the possession of happiness, tranquility, gratitude and awe, in the life of a revived sinner; one who has been resuscitated and brought back to life, to live in newness of life. That person is now a new creation indeed. Do you follow the flow of events here? I trust you do.

"For by one offering He [Christ] hath perfected forever them that are santified." Hebrews 10:14. The believer is now made perfect, sanctified or set apart forever for Himself. We can easily shout glory to God! The control or rain is taken back out of our hands and handed back to the Maker. Saint Augustine in *"The City of God"* showed us in a nut shell our position before God. He stated: "It was since man forsook God by pleasing himself that he was handed over to

38 Himself, and because he did not obey God he could not obey himself. Hence came the more obvious misery where man does not live as he wishes to live."1 The City of God. p343.

What our father Adam wanted was mastery over self and dominion over the creation butwhat he got permanently and instantly was servitude and hardship in managing himself and the creation. Needless to say we inherited what he got. We want to do it our way but it does not work and will never work to bring us into the harbour of rest. We must relinquish the reins to the able hands of our Saviour. Our best efforts will only aid in bringing a depreciating value. We cannot win on our own, pure and simple, we need the guiding Hands of the Almighty. It is not a few of us who have discovered that fact and many are discovering it every day throughout the world, not only by ordinary people like me but by brilliant minds who have explored it all. Some have turned their microscopes inwardly and their telescopes outward and are in awe of what they see. Their conclusion in a nut shell: *God the Great Creator."* This conclusion and surrender brings the desired rest they sought all their lives. Power at last is found in humility and surrender to God.

Can the revisionist topple the Christian's experiences and convictions? They can only try. That is the extent of their effectiveness on the minds of the responsible and the prudent; here they have a big uphill battle and a bigger problem still to try to make their doctrine count for something. They are still dancing when the music stops because they do not know that they are beaten. Theirs's a sad state and their aspiration and cunning ends ultimately on a sad note, a dissonant note. They have gambled and lost; they have lost everything by tampering with the truth.

CHAPTER 5

PEACE, THE MOST SOUGHT AFTER POSSESSION

Isaiah 26:3. *"Thou wilt keep him in perfect peace, whose mind is stayed on thee because he trusteth in thee."* He will keep you in perfect peace and the peace of God which passeth all understanding is the Christian's stronghold. This is the foundation of the Christian's life. It is on this basis that they build their lives. They will have no effectiveness working in the kingdom of God until this most valuable commodity is personalized. God gives this gift to those with a repentant and contrite heart. After receiving this gift, that person is commissioned to be an effective worker in the Kingdom of God because they are not labouring under the guilt of sin,

39 nor carrying that burden which sin inflicts. The weight is lifted and they are free to run the race which is set before them.

This epoch in one's life is the line of demarcation that separates them from worry and anxiety and propels them into one of everlasting bliss. It is this possession more than anything else that draws the line between the unbeliever and the believer, the saint and the sinner. This is the visible mark of one's conversion. An observable distinction carried by the recipient and observed by those around. A light now shines where there was darkness; a glow is emitted in place of gloominess. In essence, a new life has sprung forth and everyone is affected by it. Even the blind can see it eventually because the love and affection is transferred to that person. One sinner has fallen in love with his Redeemer and is forgiven and now rejoices and that is the sum total of conversion.

John Wesley, that great hymn writer was out preaching to the lost and himself did not experience the peace of God. I would not speculate whether he was saved in this state or not but if you are not ready to meet your Maker in death then maybe you are not saved. The story is that he was returning from the United States back to Britain after a time on the mission field when a violent storm erupted and the ship on which he was, looked dismally lost. He was terrified of dying and there he met some Moravian missionaries returning to Britain singing and praising God as though they were on a picnic. John Wesley himself was at his wits end, terrified of dying and spoke with them and then came to know the Lord in earnest and found the peace which is the hallmark of all Christians.

The essence of a person is his soul and not his body and as such nothing or anyone can touch that soul. No circumstance can diminish the peace which is not man made or conjured by oneself but pours like a river from God by the Holy Spirit. Our peace rest securely in the hands of God. This is our surety that we belong when we rest in this assurance. Know this truth truthfully, dearly beloved and embrace it delightfully.

As the saying goes, the proof of the pudding is not in the looks but in the eating. Regardless of how dainty and seductive it looks, until you have that first bite you cannot tell whether it is good or not. If one is not willing to give his or her life for Christ let alone face death naturally on their own without any fear, then maybe just maybe that person is not born again. If the light does not shine maybe there is no battery, no power source.

These two verses: Isaiah 26:3 "Thou wilt keep him in perfect peace, whose mind is stayed on thee because he truseth in thee."

and Philippians 4:7: "And the peace of God which passeth all understanding, shall keep your hearts and minds through Christ Jesus" harmonises to produce the most glorious song the Christian has ever known. Having possessed the peace which is

40 promised equips the Christian who now is well fortified to face all the vicissitudes of this life. They can suffer any hardships, disabilities and wait patiently for their turn to enter into their permanent rest. If nothing else, this one piece of evidence is enough to set us apart from the world. The Christian is unperturbed when everyone else is running wild in times of crisis because their faith is anchored in Christ Jesus. They know that the outcome of every event is controlled by the Almighty God. The Christian's life is likened to a controlled burn. A bystander might be alarmed at that fire but the firemen have it under control, no one needs to be alarmed who knows what the outcome will be.

When I was in property management, one Sunday as I came home from Church the phone rang and a tenant said that he was giving notice to leave and as soon as I hung up, I received another call for the same reason from another tenant. For a struggling landlord that would be enough to set my head ablaze but thank God it did not faze me. As a matter fact, it worked out for my good for I rented both apartments for more money. God be praised.

In spite of this trust and peace, the Christian at times walk a tight rope not feeling as securely walking as if he were on *terra fermi*. It is so because we are still in the flesh but as we walk, we imagine a perfect future state where the brilliant light from so hopeful a vision casts a deep shadow on the present status quo. We shall be changed and given a glorious body one which is not subjected to sickness and suffering. Oh glorious morning, after the sufferings here, we awaken to see our Jesus; that will be a glorious day indeed. Then our faith will be turned into sight and our pain into joy unspeakable. What a wonderful day that will be when my Jesus Isee.

Yet the Christian's view of seeing, is not esoteric; confined to a few narrow elite but open and can be seen by any who will accept the invitation to: "Come." During Christ's day on earth, He did not surround Himself with the elites; noblemen and women, He embraced everyone from a fisherman to a woman of the street, from embezzlers to blind beggars. Christ was and is for everyone at all times and still reaches out to every station in society. We find however, that the poor and the downtrodden find a greater friendship in Him. Some with only a mat as earthly possession find it easier to be set free from the burden of sin and guilt and rejoices in that freedom more than some carrying cumbersome baggage.

None who has had the experience of being set free from sin, made to see when they were blind, will testify otherwise, we all know that the prescription when filled, works. Peaceful living and glorious dying are the *forte* of such who possess this blessing, this glorious hope: "Christ in us the hope of glory" is substantive.

41 Someone has said: "*The roots of our joy are in His grace rather than in our goods, His mercy rather than in our money, His worth rather than in our wealth.*" Of course, men have come to disdain the very things they literally killed themselves to possess, because instead of those things bringing them peace which they hoped for, they brought miseries and death. How warped are our thinking at times. The roots of our joy then, are all about Him and not about us. We ought not to lose sight of this fact. The self is unimportant and needs to be humbled and sometimes crucified and be put out of the way so we can see the Almighty God high and lifted up as Isaiah saw Him.

In all likelihood, we are placing our trust in passing fancies instead of in the stability and worth of the Almighty God; who is length, width, height and depth. He is simple unfathomable. Our priorities are misplaced and may God help us to realign them before there is no further chance to connect with Him. For the little time we have here upon earth and for what is left for some of us aging senior citizens, we cannot squander any more time listlessly. We must put all on the altar of sacrifice and surrender fully to Him. God help us to see it clearly. The restlessness and wonderings that envelops our lives are because of unhappiness for the most part; it is an effort to fill a void that has to be met but as St Augustine said: *"Our hearts are restless until they rest in God."* God alone is our resting place, God is where home is and until we return home we will forever be wondering and lonely. More than ever, God is calling His children home and He is using myriad means of reaching us. He is employing all the means because the time is short. He is even at the door and I hope you who are reading this will open up to Him. Why would you wait or linger when there is danger in doing so. This moment is all that you have, you are not promised another breath, and if this were your last, use it to ask for mercy and connect deeper with Him.

Peter therefore, says; in light of the nearness to the end of all things, we should watch unto prayer. This is my state; I am watching and praying, for I can feel His nearness and more so, the nearness of His second appearing.

Have you noticed how so many today are running after riches, temporal riches that is but are still very poor toward the things of God. They have exhausted all of their resources to furnish their dwelling places but I believe that God gives back temporal goods to those intending only temporal ends as such. Their only reward is here and they are receiving their rewards in full in this temporary dwelling place. There will be nothing left to come as rewards after this life. Their next abode will leave them destitute, needing even a cup of water and there will be none. They would have invested all in this life and lost.

42 It would be fitting here to insert "Pascal's Wager." It reads like this: *"If one bets that there is no God and wins he wins nothing but if he loses he loses everything."* Pascal is not throwing out this reasoning as an intimidation tool or to coerce anyone but to let them know the grave danger they embrace in objecting to so much evidence which supports God's existence. Psalm 19 states: *"The heavens declare the glory of God; and the firmament showeth His handy work."* Now you will convince yourself that this is

man's wisdom or this portion is written by man and all the other Scriptures are written also by man, so why believe it too.

The Word or the Scriptures are authentically God's word. The Bible says that they are God breathed. God simply directed men to write the words that are written. The Word has been changing lives for centuries and continues to change lives even as you read this. It has so changed men and women that some have turned their backs on great wealth in favour of serving God and winning souls for the Kingdom. It has removed drunken men from the gutter and placed them in good standing in society and restored them to their families. Billy Sunday was confronted by a drunkard who asked him if he knew what his little girl might like for Christmas. Yes! Billy said: *"A sober dad."* A word from this man of God changed this family's life forever. How glorious is that. If we are led by the Spirit of God then we must walk in the Spirit of God and as such our conversation will emit a sweet aroma. Our very presence will be attractive.

The testimony of this particular drunkard is rather hilarious. This drunkard testified after his conversion that the Lord has turned beer to chairs and table in his house. The money that formerly went to buying beer has now been used to furnish a table and chairs for his dwelling. A small miracle you might say but there are countless drunkards who cannot break the habit on their own. It takes a miracle to clean up many and to change the lives of the downtrodden. I was in that state as a young man and God changed me for good. I know that I would not be encouraging men and women to come to Christ and experience the change; I know that I would be dead a long time ago. God be praised that I began trusting in Him as a young man of twenty two.

If you do not believe the Bible, then you are inconsistent with your own self. You choose to believe some history and not others because a great portion of the Bible or the Scripture is history. This history is recorded by men as directed by the Holy Spirit.

When the truth has gotten hold of you, you will believe it and it will set you free and only then will you be free.

Who is it in the Western world that would not know of Jesus? No one; except those whodeliberately push Him out of their thoughts. They are therefore, wilfully ignorant.

43 A Christian wife said that after her husband refused to believe in the Lord Jesus Christ as his Saviour, she began deliberately to treaty him especially kindly, more so than she would normally because she realizes that this life will be the only one in which he will see or have any more enjoyment. When he crosses over into eternity he will have lost any further chance for a good life. His place of abode from then on will be torment. It will literally be Hell. The chance for change of mind will be lost forever. It is easy enough now to bow in humbly submission to God but after death it will be impossible to do so. Why would anyone not do this, knowing as they do that life is fleeting and tomorrow is unknown and uncertain.

Failure to acknowledge Christ as Lord is to neglect our own future and ruin any chance of a blessed eternity. He is who He says He is: "The Way, the Truth and the Life." John 14:6. A man's unbelief, his shame and ultimate demise comes because of his pride. He has said it, if not verbally but implicitly: *"I will not have this man to rule over me,"* that is his decision pure and simple. He is in one camp or the other but he cannot remain neutral. Christ said; you cannot serve two masters; for you will love one and hate the other.

Can we see here then that while He is sovereign, yet He has given us a will of our own to choose as He did at the beginning with Adam? Adam chose to disobey His command. We too are free to receive His message of Grace and Mercy or to reject it outright as worthless and needless. Here a man exercises his rights when he chose to reject Christ for should the Lord bound him, it would be coercion. The Lord pleads with a man and the Holy Spirit witnesses to him to draw him to a saving knowledge but many have still turned Him away. Although many have good intensions, yet procrastination is a thief and will rob you of your birthright and destined you to a place of torment. Today is the day of salvation, act now and do not put it off.

One man stated that he travelled a different road to work because he did not want to read the sign: "Ye must be born again." The truth can be troubling at times when we are bent on doing our own thing. The truth is, no one needs insurance whether on your car or on your home as long as you do not have an accident or a fire. Home insurance does not keep the fire from our houses; we buy it so that in case there is a fire our loss is not unsustainable. It is against such an event that we pay the expensive premiums. Should there be no reckoning after death, we would all be home free; we could all live and have a splendid time, we would just all need to keep the golden rule that would be good enough. It is the resurrection and summation again after death that is troubling. At that time a man or a woman without Christ as his advocate is simply on his own and there is only one plea he can enter into and that is "Guilty."

44 St. Augustine rightly said: *"Christ as God is the country to which we go; Christ as human is the way by which we go."* Christ as human or in human flesh is the road to God. He is man's identification or introduction to God. Without Christ coming in the flesh we would nototherwise be able to communicate and know our Father. His existence would forever transcend our understanding and knowledge. We would always be setting up idols to the *"Unknown God"* still delighting in a religion that is not salvific. We can easily say that most religion will not afford a worshipper a lift off come resurrection day. The ostrich will have more lift than them all. The only religion which will lift you off this planet is Christianity. Christianity is the only veritable religion, and all the others are vacuities. Embrace Christianity and prove it to be so. When the Lord returns, there will be no power on earth which will be able to keep us down as Christians. We will be off at the sound of the trumpet. This is our future, believe it.

CHAPTER 6

GOD'S LAWS ARE ABSOLUTES

God's laws are absolutes; from the seemingly smallest to the weightiest. All of them are indeed laws which we would do well to observe such as the law of gravity and all the others we live by daily and yet take for granted. There is no simple law, they are all supernatural, because they were designed or put in place by God Himself. We live or die by them but we cannot challenge their validity. We must not minimize or adulterate any to fit our situation or taste. God's word stands like an everlasting fortress and no man can annul it. *"His truth marches on."* We do well only when we embrace His laws and follow and acknowledge His truths. We will not survive outside of His directions. He is the guiding light and to dwell in security we need that Light, only then will we walk securely.

Living outside of this light, blights our perceptions and even stifle our intelligence. One might think nothing of living outside of Christ and feel nothing of the effects of the neglect but much is lost and everyday a little more is lost on the journey. A constant ruin is experienced without any renewal. The Christian on the other hand lives and learn even amidst great difficulties but we never lose or are we losers. Our victory is fixed and will be realized as sure as night follows day. There is no power which will be able to thwart that outcome. We shall come out the other end as fine gold.

45 I have met them, I have seen them and I am one myself; being put through the fiery furnace and yet we come out winners. Not by our own strength but by the power which is vested in us through the Holy Spirit. We are endued with an indomitable spirit and that is our strength. We simply refuse to allow the problems of life to subdue our will and to subvert our triumph. We will not succumb to boredom; instead we use the difficulties as a spring board to propel us to higher heights. We are not defeatists but have learned to master our problems, making lemonade out of lemons. We embrace a winning attitude not hopefully but knowingly. We now know that we know.

Soren Kierkegaard, Danish philosopher and writer states: *"Boredom is the root of all evil- the despairing refusal to be oneself."* In this thought lies the underlying fact that we are all gifted individuals with great potentials but few of us see our full potential. Not many of us have the courage and the fortitude to explore and fulfill that possibility to a great degree. When we are not fully engaged there are many distractions vying for our attention and these distractions are carrying us off course and sidelining our worth every time. A diligent and focused perspective is the key to one's success. Keeping focused on the business at hand and never letting up or being sidelined by distractions. The Christians target is Christ Himself, honouring and living for Him.

He goes on to say: *"There is nothing with which everyman is so afraid as getting to know how enormously much he is capable of doing and becoming."* When we carry out a full examination of our true selves we can relate to this statement that we can be much more than we presently are. This statement rocks my core also as I read it. Even as a man in my seventies I am realizing that that is a potential that is virtually untouched and I am curious to investigate and explore it. I want to see where it will take me and when it will end. There are so much to be involved in that one should scarcely be bored. Get engaged and see in the next little while what you can make of yourself. Don't be afraid to explore your full potential. Try pursuing it and find out where it will lead you. Together we will see.

To contextualize, here we have the source of blessing as copious as Grace which makes us happy in hope and yet men everywhere still seek a fulfilled life elsewhere; outside of Christ. Outside of the confines of Grace and its attendant source there is no lasting happiness. We can try to get on without the Source of power and blessings but we will not journey far. We will soon be exhausted by our own energy and surrender eventually as we all do without this power. God's laws, God's commandments are the Christians sources of enjoyment and fruitful living, we must embrace His dictates exuberantly for them to have their full impact in our lives. Exhausted and ruined are the conditions of many in their search and suddenly they realized that someone somewhere might be right and they cried out and obtained mercy and help in

46 their distresses. That story is echoed many hundreds of times over as testimonies of the power of the Gospel which alone can transform lives and satisfy the desires for meaning in their lives are repeated daily. God alone satisfies. Nothing else comes close.

The Gospel, the Good news, the Word, is the power of God unto salvation. You will not have an awareness of your sins until the Word has had an impact on your life. It might appear as a cruel task master but upon yielding you will grow to cherish and love it. It is power; it is the antidote for all your maladies. You will not know its power until you surrender to its appeal. It will be like learning a new language, only that this will be easier and much more rewarding. The language of love will be instilled in your memory almost instantaneously. Forgiveness as a way of life will be manageable, and it will produce great benefits, freeing you up to function as you should. Acknowledging God's laws and submitting to them are of paramount importance in navigating the new course. The delight that the new behaviour brings however, will be more than you ever dreamt of. Now you have a connection to heaven which evaded you previously. This richness in knowing Christ will excite you beyond your wildest imagination.

When a person has the witness in themselves, they seek to correct and shun sin not condone it. They take the Word of God seriously and believe what it says and not doubt its veracity. They simply submit. He does not treat the Bible as a circus board where some things are enjoyable and others are left alone. They must embrace every word as truth and the authority of God. Hopeful thinking is dispensed with, at the intake of the Word. We cannot battle sin on our own terms, no matter how strong and spiritual we think we are. If sin resides in us still, as it must until it is forgiven, then we are fighting a losing battle. It will give us neither respite nor freedom no matter how hard we try. Many great believers have come to realize that we cannot fight sin and overcome it. It will torment and harass us all the days of our lives. Our lives must be purged of this malignant tenant once and for all. It must be eradicated for good and the new life is infused in its place. Sin cannot be operated on; it has to be removed completely by the act of remission. Christ Jesus died on Calvary's cross to do just that, if we but come to Him and ask for forgiveness. So now, instead of sin having dominion over us, now are we inflicted with a new demand on our lives; a new urge to do good and to align our lives with righteousness. Such is our state after conversion.

There is something which I could not tell you about because although I wrote about it, I did not experience it. It is the preparation to go out of this life. It is death. The new life enables us to face death honourably and gracefully. We are not afraid of the word death. Each of us will meet our Waterloo but the Christian's Waterloo is faced differently. Today the nineteenth day of July 2017, I got the news of yesterday's CT scan at the Hospital. My doctor called to say I have lung cancer. It was noon when he called and I have not told anybody yet. It is now 7:37

47 P.M. and I have not disclosed the news as yet. How will my wife and daughter take the news, I don't know but I know how I received it. Next birthday, April 3oth, I will be eighty years old and it certainly would be odd if after preparing others to meet their Maker I shied away from meeting Him. I am being honest with you; I have taken it just as any other news. It is not even as shocking as when I hear of someone else's diagnosis.

If it be that the Lord is calling me home so be it. Right now I am not sure if I will be asking Him for more time. I have already divest myself of this earthly dwelling place and am working and looking forward to my eternal home and this was long before my home going news. The loose ends have been coming together wonderfully and I believe it will not take me long to close those ends. This was a diversion which I believe I owe my readers and perhaps by the time you read this book I will be on the other side; I mean with my Father. This book is completed; I am now only revising it. The last chapter 20 is already finished.

Every time I speak to people about their salvation I know whether they are believers or not. I hear equally often that I should not judge but judgement is discernment. If we lack discernment we will be deceived. Just going to church or having a suit of clothes does not make us Christians. We must follow God's word implicitly. We must recognize that God has not changed and will execute judgement and righteousness eventually. Living for Christ is not a casual encounter but a total commitment and a lifetime endeavour. The Lord calls us to a life of sacrifice and total commitment. Taking the narrow road and despising the broad road. We have to forsake all and follow Him. We must not try to give his commands a new meaning. Too often when we present the word and its import, we hear that that is your interpretation. Where the word is clear, there can be no different interpretation but just what it says. Certain rules are laid down not to be repealed, not even by God Himself let alone feeble and insignificant humans.

If we must follow God, it is obligatory to walk with His son Jesus Christ. We cannot have one without the other. It is recorded one hundred and forty four times where Jesus commands us to follow Him. Following Jesus is not simply naming His name but doing the things He has commanded. He Himself has said if you are my disciples then you must keep my commandments. His commandments are not grievous; Come learn of me He said, my yoke is easy and my burden is light. Jesus gives a song as we travel life's road because as He said, His yoke is easy. When we are yoked to Jesus He does most of the pulling, personally I will not have it any other way. It is like most of the things we do today, they are automated; cutting the grass, lifting a load and so on. We know what it is to have most of our loads lifted for us.

48 We will live or die by the laws or commandments but we cannot ever hope to void or diminish them in any way. We live in certain boldness and pride about our status instead of bowing in humble submission to the Word. The veracity of the Word will judge us most certainly, there is no escaping. God has spoken and His words stand.

Today we hear of "Alternative Facts or Alternative Truths." There can be but one truth or one fact. We must not allow ourselves to be manipulated by anyone no matter whom, or what they call themselves. They come in all shapes and sizes but they are only deceivers seeking your eternal souls. Selling yourself short is something you cannot afford to do. A person hope to gain from a sale not lose from it and selling your soul even for all the gold in Fort Knox is still not getting true value. Jesus said in Matthew 16:26: *"For what is a man profited, if he shall gain the whole world, and lose his soul?* Your eternal soul is priceless.

Many today who are supposed to be in the camp are doing just that. They are gambling with their souls for wealth. Wealth or possession has taken the place of godly living and many are busy enjoying themselves to the expense of famished souls. It is a poor choice now and poorer still they will realize on that great day. In eternity, everything will be magnified a billion times and our sights will have become the clearest. No longer will we see things dimly but everything will be made crystal clear. Those in Hell will see why they could not be admitted to heaven and those in heaven will know that any hardship or deprivation was all for our good. To be present in His presence diminishes a billion fold, every hardship suffered while here on earth.

Many poor choices are being made every day but some are with irreversible consequences. A person may sacrifice his or her health in favour of wealth. They neglect to eat properly or to add exercise to the lifestyle and as a result suffer some physical disability and live to regret it but a soul dying without Christ will realize at the Judgement day that they will have lost everything eternally. That will be an irreversable loss. I might have said it somewhere here already but it warrants repeating and my prayer is that none who reads this book will suffer such a loss.

This book is written especially to encourage you dear believer who are still wondering whether you have made the right decision or not by following Christ. You might not be sure whether you have made the right decision and are on the border line of quitting but listennow. You might not be enjoying your Christian life because you have not fully committed to Christ. You are not giving to the work of Christ as you should and are not attending the services as you must and so on and so on; therefore, you are not enjoying the prosperity and fruitfulness that a child of God is promised. I would advise you to get in the work of God and immerse yourself and you will know the difference between serving and observing.

49 When a bird is caged it is restless and no doubt bored for it was designed to soar in the heavens. Flight is the bird's delight and life in the fullest sense. Likewise, a born again Christian (as if there is any other) must be fully involved in God's Kingdom to be entirely free. He or she must be engaged in whatever it is that that person can do. Some in witnessing, some praying, some

giving and whatever else; although all of the aforementioned can be carried out by a single believer, all are our responsibilities.

Building up the body of Christ is something we hear about quite often from the pulpit and yet many times we are not instructed how we can accomplish that command. Oftentimes we go to church and settle in a rigid routine and never hear a sermon which shakes us out of our complacency. We read the scriptures and settle for some parts of it as truth and dogma but fail to connect the dots. It takes a Preacher who is about feeding his flock to make the connection for us at times, because on our own, sometimes we will not see what the passage is intending to teach us.

I hereby draw this portion of Scriptures to your attention: Hebrews 13:15. *"By him therefore let us offer the sacrifice of praise to God continually, that is, the fruit of our lips giving thanks to his name."* My! If we read, underline and memorize this passage and exercise this command regularly we would be sure we are fulfilling the command of this passage in its entirety. We would certainly be pleased with ourselves and can feel satisfy that we are serving God as we should. But for the next verse, we would be off the hook surely. It is the next verse which is doing the shaking. It shakes us so hard and our bones are out of joint.

Verse 16 reads: *"But to do good and to communicate forget not: for with such sacrifices God is well pleased."* The first verse deals with us and how we love to think of ourselves as the one who deserves the best of everything. A new car, a new house, a new suit, a new dress and so on and the list never ends. All this seems good and well until the conjunction chips in. BUT! To do good. Well doing good moves from self and is extended to others. To do good we must stretch out our hands and reach out to others. There are a million and one ways to reach out to others. When you stop to speak to the person cleaning the plaza, give him a tract, when you stop to give a hand out to the panhandler and have a chat and hand a tract, we are doing good. When we connect with someone who is bereaved and help with some form of financial assistance, we are doing good.

We do good to everyone except ourselves. How many are like the old Scrooge, miserly and miserable but look at the new Scrooge when he had a change of heart and began to be charitable. He could literally jump over the moon, he became light and free and in so short a time he was transformed into a delightful person. The second portion of verse 16 states that

50 must communicate. We are not only called upon to be charitable but to be evangelists. Communicating here is signifying not just small talk but more importantly, communicating our faith; sharing the Gospel of Christ.

Francis of Assisi once said: *"We must preach the Gospel and if possible use words."* Our lives should be living testimonies to others and we must back it up with words also. Words of comfort, words of encouragement and words of light and wisdom; words have the Pygmalion effect never be stingy with it. Formulate kind thoughts and use those words to comfort others.

We had a very useful diversion and it was necessary, for it is instruction we seek if we are a part of the body of Christ. We need to grow. So let me get back to encouraging you to becoming a more fruitful Christian.

I could liken a child of God not living to his or her full potential as a Rolls Royce or GE engine sitting on the shop floor, being polished and dusted each day; beautiful perhaps to look at but not doing what it was designed to do. They were designed to hum in the sky transporting people and goods from one part of the globe to the other. Why should any of us be as we are, useless and unproductive after being commissioned to "Go."

What on earth can be more liberating than those engines doing what they were designed to do. The great Rolls Royce and GE engines, unleashing their powers in the open sky, they are testaments to the creativity of man; his genius and enterprising spirit. No wonder we feel liberated to do as we please, but we are so wrong. We are attached; we are interconnected to each other and have our accountability to our Maker.

Just as soon as we disconnect with God, that is when we begin to decline or make our dangerous descent to ruin. We cannot sustain ourselves without the guiding hand of the Almighty God; neither will we prosper without that sustaining hand. We do what we do only by the common grace extended to all. We are kept by His Mighty hand and yet we do not acknowledge it. At times we attribute our so called successes to our own ingenuity and skills. Man is woefully stubborn and will not give honour where honour belongs. He would rather usurp that credit. Our nations are sick and disjointed so also are individuals as they disconnect with their Maker. The whole world groans under the burden of sin and we see the results of sin in our time as the conclusion of the matter draws near. In spite of the manifestation of evil about us some religions will still say there is no such thing as sin. Yet they claim to worship the same God as we do.

It is written, righteousness exalts a nation and sin is a reproach to any people. When our morals are corrupt and distorted we will bring upon ourselves the disapproval of the Almighty

51 God. He will inevitably judge and punish us and in many cases give us up to our own sinful devices which will draw us into the abyss. We may believe it or we may choose to ignore it but the laws will play out to our destruction eventually. Many have broken loose from what they consider a tyrannical Master. They do not want to be dictated to. Freedom reigns in their lives greater than a command to repent and return to righteousness. They cry out to be free. They want laws which will give them licences to sin and they are getting such licences. The law makers will relent and allow many ungodly practices but God's law does not change, it has the same clout notwithstanding man's wavering. We turn a deaf ear to God's word and pretend that it is worthless but nothing changes, notwithstanding our attitudes toward Him. We

all will be called to give an account of our deeds; whether those deeds are good or evil.

I have watched them march to defy God and to trample on His word, celebrating as though they had won a great victory over a tyrannical enemy but in all of this I can say that God is merciful and indeed is not willing that any should perish for He would consume them then. He is truly longsuffering and will even allow a person to self-destruct; giving them enough rope asthey need to hang themselves.

In all of this, the Lord is laughing; Psalm 2:4 says:"He that sitteth in the heavens shall laugh: the Lord shall have them in derision." They think that they are mocking God but the Lord has the last laugh. He it is who will be laughing at them and then their plight will be an awful one. Imagine the Judge finding one in contempt of court and says: "Guard! Get him out of my sight." You are whisked away and locked up and the Judge laughs silently. "You son-of- a barbarian, go enjoy yourself now."

Now returning to the subject of our stance as Christians. Many will give the Lord a little of everything but keep most of their time and earnings for themselves. They are two timers. It does not work that way. Jesus has said we have to deny ourselves and follow Him. Has he got the right to demand such a submission? He submitted Himself even to the death of the cross to save us and is therefore worthy of our highest trust and devotion. He walked the most notorious road in the world for us. He walked the *"Via Dolorosa"* the way of the cross to buy our salvation and that is enough for me. He has bought my salvation and I will serve Him because He is worthy of my best. Thank God in my state now, I do not have to rush to mend the fences for I have been diligent in doing so ever since I embraced the new life.

I interrupt every few sentences to interject a warning and hope that by the end of this book you might see your responsibility and make a meaningful response. We cannot face the judgement alone, we need an advocate and we have that advocate in the person of Jesus Christ the Righteous to plead on our behalf. We have no standing on our own. The big question will be

52 "What have you done with my Son" How will we answer that question. The truth is, if we have rejected Him there will only be one response from God. *"Depart."* Depart is a word that many so called Christians will be hearing because they are two-timers. They have one foot in the world and one in the Church. I mentioned before that setting sail we cannot have each foot in a boat, we must decide and get into one completely.

It does not take much of a person to follow Christ but it takes that entire person. We have to make a clean break from this world or else we might be wasting our time. We do not want to hear "Depart" on that faithful day.

There will be wailing and gnashing of teeth, but to no avail. Too late it will be. Elizabeth Barrett Browning writes:

> Earth's crammed with heaven
> And every common bush afire with God
> But only he who sees, takes off his shoes,
> The rest, sit round it and pluck blackberries.

We need to see and in order to see we need to open our eyes and our minds to the eternal even as we struggle with the temporal. The visible are the temporal and the invisible are the eternal and that is where life begins in earnest. Death is not the end but the door into the eternal and we would do well to see that as truth. We have become more and more blinded to the eternal because of the earthly distractions which envelopes us more and more. We are grossly enamored with the brick and mortar and tinsel of this age to see clearly. We need to take a long walk and sift things out, once and for all. "...Be ye reconciled to God." 2 Corinthians 5:20.

The sky could be falling and some of us would not see it. Everyone is busy on some gadget or other or have our ears plugged. We have made a resolute determination to shut out a great deal of our existence. We will not see with our spiritual eyes because we are distracted. Whatever we can feel and touch and see are temporal and what we cannot see except with our spiritual eyes are eternal and substantive. The temporal is fading and will vanish as a cloud but the eternal is coming to replace it and it is permanent. It is God's word that states it and it is true.

We mentioned earlier the power of the Rolls Royce and the GE engines and we know that those engines are no good sitting on a factory floor and being paraded as the best engines in

53 the world when they do not get to do what the engineers designed them to do. Likewise, we will not soar until we unshackle ourselves from untruth, half-truths and outright lies and embrace the Truths of God's word. That truth is not found under every rock or in every tree, it is found in the inspired word of God and it is worth searching for. There is a search and a find and you will know when you have pounced upon that Truth. The truth is liberating and intoxicating. You will literally be swept off your feet as when you meet someone you are enchanted with. We are living in turbulent times and we would do well to know what we believe and know that it is true. The truth is unchanging and is as old as the hills or creation itself. Turbulent times are with us and we have been warned that there will be false prophets.

Many have come running saying God is dead, some say there is no God others are saying God's word is changing and a host of other falsities. It is quite easy to settle on a belief or a sea of beliefs as though it were the Gospel. Some arguments are laid out so wonderfully that they seem plausible but are spurious. Most truths are made plain for us to see yet many escape our understanding and will have to be expounded by the Ministers of the Gospel. I have listened to a sermon recently where one man insinuated that the Old Testament teachings are obsolete. We do not have to adhere to them and as such he has shown us a tattoo on his arm although forbidden by Leviticus 19:28. *"Ye shall not make any cuttings in your flesh for the dead, nor print any marks upon you: I am the Lord."* Would we then throw away the Ten Commandments? Are we now free to indulge in any sin because we are under the dispensation of Grace? God forbid. Men are routinely seeking to undermine God's authority and if it displeases me, then how much more must God be? Isaiah 5:25 states: *"…For all this his anger is not turned away, but his hand is stretched out still."* God will never be pleased with wrongdoings, nor will he wink at sin but in spite of our waywardness and sinfulness, He still pleads with us to turn. Our only hope of escaping His anger and terror is our turning to repentance. Until our hearts are made aright and anew, we will not see God in His righteousness and worship Him as the Omnipotent One.

Man might live by making laws justifying his indulgences but where God forbids such practices he will be held accountable. In Psalm 119: 89. We read. *"For ever, O Lord, thy word is settled in heaven."* Man cannot annul God's laws; they remain intact for ever and ever. A person who commits sin any sin, no matter how trivial or heinous, remains a sinner and is subject to the punishment according to God's law but if he or she confesses and turns away from that sin, then that person is in a new category. He is forgiven and exonerated as though he had not committed that sin. He or she is now justified before God and made a new creature or is *"born again"* as the Bible terms it.

54 To the Church in Corinth, Paul writes: *"Know ye not that the unrighteous shall not inherit the kingdom of God? Be not deceived. Neither fornicators nor idolaters, nor adulterers, nor effeminate, nor abusers of themselves with mankind, and such were some of you but ye are washed, but ye are sanctified…"* I Corinthians 5: 9 & 11. It is a new day after repentance for any person. They are now redeemed. Their iniquities have been washed away by the Blood of Christ and they bear their sins no more. Christ bore it for us on the cross of Calvary; that is history.

It is a new page they have to write on from then on. The old things have passed away and all things have become new; that's how it is in God's sight, for He has forgotten our sins. He has dumped the past records in the depths of the sea and remembers them no more. As far as God is concerned, He cannot remember a time when we were not clean. That is amazing, if ever I can use that word. The Lord cannot remember a time when Trevor Turner was a sinner. I have to say: "My God! This is hard to comprehend." There are other things which I will never be able to understand also, so I will leave this here. On the contrary, we must remember that God has not forgotten any sin which He has not forgiven. They remain on the books. We can dream on and hope for a good outcome but if the least of our sins are still on the books, then we are forever outside of the pearly gates. No sin can enter there.

There are too many pacifists in our pulpits ready to make peace with the enemy at all cost. They have not drawn the line between good and evil, recognizing that God is absolutely righteousness.

We the redeemed have now no record, we are free and clear in His sight. If anyone can describe a scene more refreshing and liberating than that, I do not want to hear it. This is the ultimate experience, to have our sins forgiven, the penalty removed and the burden and weight released. The only appropriate words we can use to express the sublimity of this reality are: "To God be the glory, great things He has done." Christ Jesus has set us free by His blood and we are free indeed. We do not have to be coerced into believing such a statement, we experience the freedom; it comes naturally to settle in as a great calm in our souls. It is part of the package of belonging to Christ.

"Keep calm and carry on" was a phrase which Sir. Winston Churchill coined during the stormy blast over London by the Germans during the Second World War. It was an effective strategy which worked very well during those stressful times. Nicketa Cruschev once jumped up on the work bench in an ammunition factory and cried out to the workers that whether

they worked or hid under the benches the effect of war would get to them, so it is well to be productive in

55 such times. These are motivational strategies used to keep men and women moving in times of great distresses and without such brilliant minds finding ways to motivate the discouraged, the outcome of wars could be different many times. We are in warfare also and we also need to be motivated and kept buoyant and as such the Scriptures serve as our motivator. We need to read it daily to have the Author speak to us as we march on this pilgrim pathway. We need a daily dose of the Scripture to keep us strong and vigilant; that is the only way we shall overcome the trials and temptations that beset us. The Word is our source of strength.

A lot of what we see and hear in life is nothing but illusions and distractions hallow sounds vying for our attentions and most will eventually swallow us up like the quicksand if we are not careful to differentiate between what is real and what is false. Vigilance is the operative or the watch word in the believer's life. We have to watch and pray so that we are not sucked in. There is a grave danger in careless living. We must tighten our boot straps and be ready to do battle every minute of every day. A trained soldier we must remain and on guard always.

Some of us live our lives and are consumed by illusionary things that have little meaning and substance and we disappear from the face of the earth as though we had never been here. We have made no lasting mark on society. Let us go down as those who have been helpful, living and lending a hand to the oppressed, the disenfranchised and the indigent. Show it, not just say it. Remembering that doing good is with a stretched out hand, reaching out to help others just as God has His hand stretched out ready to assist us also. Let this attitude be our consuming passion and we will have satisfied the greatest commission. "Go ye".

CHAPTER 7

LIVE PURPOSEFULLY

A purposeful life lies not in the pursuit of things, accreditation and pleasures without an added value or a spiritual dimension to it. When we take stock and consider what it is that we are getting out of our pursuit, then we can know if we are not just chasing pipe dreams or whether we have something substantive. Such deliberate thoughts will bring a wealth of difference to our health and happiness now and in the years to come. Our actions now set the stage for well-being and happiness in the years to come. As mature adults we must live Biblically anchored. Many things that are not in themselves sinful are not permissible for the Christian to indulge in. They are too numerous to mention here but there is one thing which is clear and that is, we are

56 to stay clear of the world; we must not be too attached to its allurements and indulgences. The distinction has to be clear enough that everyone will know whose we are.

You who are reading this as a Christian know where you are, I will not need to belabour the point, and you are your own judge. We see it all around us, that many are seeking happiness in the wrong indulgences. There was a bumper stick which reads: *"He who thinks having a lot of toys bring fulfilment is already dead."* We have seen them live and we have heard their testimonies that it is all a dream. It does not bring the fulfilment they envisioned when they ruined their friendship or their health because of it. Travel lightly, give it away and fulfil the great commandment:*"It is more blessed to give than to receive."* Acts 20: 35.

Most people are busy dying and not living as they should. We indulge in vain glory and expend our energies in things that are better left alone. Things we can easily get along without, we harass ourselves to possess them so as to impress. We become the Jones' that the world seeks to catch up to. Beware of false promises for they are but that. They do not deliver as they purport to. They fall dismally short most times from what is anticipated. In most cases it is the glitter and not the gold that we get. It is all a mirage, a dream with no substance. We must all live soberly in a consumeristic society.

Know the truth and let it reign richly in every aspect of your life and you will undoubtedly reap untold benefits. Be truthful to yourself and do not be deceived by others. The deception envelopes us like a cloud and we have to untangle it from our thoughts daily.

Some have determined to compromise to the very end. There is no hope for you in the eternal scheme of things because the approbation of man is greater to you than the approbation of God. There can be no fruits without roots and the deeper the roots the more abundant the fruits. A little withered fruit at best with very little soil but good fruits require good soil. Rich alluvial soil like a good diet, supply all the nutrients and sustenance for proper growth and delicious fruits. There are too many shallow soils producing distasteful fruits. Let us be up and doing, forging a path which others can follow and the Master will be pleased that we forged. We must all desire to have an abundant entry into His presence and not to be hesitant nor ashamed for doing so little at the approach of his coming. That is where we can all be rich, rich toward God by the life we live and the things we share with others.

Fruit bearing serves here as an analogy to the greater and more weighty things of paramount importance. These things are so weighty that our very lives depend on them. Not only are our lives dependent upon them but our future and our eternity more so. Can a person afford to gamble with his soul which is of eternal worth? No! You cannot afford to gamble with it. If you come up short the cost will be everlasting regret. There will be no recourse in eternity as one

57 has now in this life. There are many regrets here and some we can mend or make amends for but after death it is forever too late. Am I using this word too often? May be but I want you to get a grip on this certainty.

Living purposefully is living above sin and sinful habits; supporting the Christian endeavours and shunning or condemning not condoning the wrongs of the world. We must learn to love the things that God loves and hate the things He hates. We must not be afraid to draw the line every time. Do not be a friend of the world, and be afraid of men's faces; be bold and truthful to all. When I just got saved and travelled in a car pool to work, the same guys we drank together with did not like that I would not leave the car to join them in the bar when they stopped for a drink. Soon after however, they knew and appreciated my stand. We were coworkers and remained friends but even the language in the car changed. They knew that God's representative was present in their midst. Most of them called me saved Trev because they saw the change. It was dramatic.

Endorsing wrongs and wrongdoers, giving ascent to their ungodly deeds as though God has stepped down a notch is profanity to the ninth degree. Ungodliness will be judged and punished and those who condone the sinner's ungodliness will also be judged and rewarded. Our religiosity is nothing but a tinkling cymbals and a sounding brass when it does not align itself with the Word of a Holy God.

To plead for tenderness where punishment is needed, for leniency where correction is needed is not charity, it is folly. Administration of truth is the most charitable of all our obligations. We administer truth so that many will be arrested from error. Beware of false prophets who are more compassionate then God Himself in their administration toward humans. They are forever changing God's commands; they are not His servants.

When one Christian fears the veracity of another Christian, something is terribly wrong. They are not in line with the truth of the Gospel. We know we malign another Christian when they get out of line and we know we ought not to but to malign one who is perfectly clean is a different kettle of fish. To shun such a one and to think of them as too pure for this world is revealing our own carnal conditions.

Worldly wisdom recommends the path of compromise every time; they do not see that God remains a just God with infinite justice. It is to these people that death to the world and burial with Christ is an experience that they are strangers to. They cannot bear even to be in the company of such believers since they are continually being convicted of their own sinfulness

58 but not to the point where they want to emulate such a believer. Rather, they would shun that one for just being what they are supposed to be; a faithful Christian, a person in whom there is no guile.

Some of us are distinctly called "Born again Christians" and are shunned at the same time for being the true Mc Coy. We are labelled Born Again Christians as though there are any other. In essence, there are no other Christians; there is this and only this brand or category. If you are not born again as Jesus declared, then you cannot wear that label "Christian." This is the very thing I have been trying to get across and that is for us to get both feet in the boat. A lot of us are hindering the work of God by being only pretenders and in name only but lack real substance. May God help us to drop the façade and come clean?

The Christian knows when he crosses the line and when he needs to get back to God and ask for forgiveness. He knows when he is out of line with His Saviour; his conscience convicts him every time he steps out of line. He will have no peace and composure until he has been forgiven, until then he remains a miserable and convicted soul. A person's real self is experienced only in Christ after liberation from sin, there is no illusion, the dream has ended and reality comes to bear upon that person. They set upon the truth and they know now that life has another dimension to it; the real and substantive dimension. They now experience this real dimension to which they truly belong.

We try to fit into the worldly system at times but we never can settle in comfortably, it is because we really do not belong to the world, we are dancing to the tune of a different drummer now. Have you noticed how you try at times to screw on the top of a bottle, or a jar, or a nut and if it does not sit just right on the container it does not work properly. In essence, it is designed to fit smugly and if the thread is cross, it does not do its job. The Christian is like that, they are like fish out of water when they are not in the will of God. c.s. Lewis says; *"He knows that he must be created for another world when he finds that he does not fit in this one."*

James tells us squarely: *"…The friendship of the world is enmity with God."* James 4:4. How unambiguous is this statement. We cannot and we must not dabble with the things of this world so as to fall in love with it. We must only be tent dwellers and not homesteaders. Our mission and vision is only a temporary abode, for we are pilgrims moving through. Ours is an upward march. This is our highest purpose in life.

Do not presume upon God's goodness

59 We presume upon the goodness of God almost totally and neglect to consider His righteous acts. Goodness is one of

His attributes and so is righteousness. The righteousness of God demands justice and as such we all must pay for our sins and that penalty is death. As in Adam we all died so in Christ we all shall be made alive. Christ death for sin is not an automatic covering for the whole world but for those who will accept His death as the covering for their sins personally and come to repentance. A repentant and a contrite heart He will not despise. He is waiting with outstretched arms still.

Will you accept the remedy for your sin?

There is no liberation from sin without conviction of sin. It follows therefore, that one cannot continue in sinful practices and call themselves believers. It is a misnomer, a contradiction of terms. You cannot have your cake and eat it also. It cannot be done; one has to choose between abiding in sin and following Christ. In summary, nothing can be fully understood without reference to Gods creation and His divine plan for that creation. His divine plan is the way back to Himself which He has made possible through the crucified One and anyone desiring to have communion with the Father must submit to Christ. He is the door through which we all must come to the Father. *"No one comes to the father but by Christ."* John 14:6.

God has not left us uninformed as to what things are and what they will be. The Bible reveals the mind of God and the state of man and the consummation of this system. It is a sign post pointing us to godly and honourable living. We can be helped if we are not taken up with our selves. We cannot be proud men and women spouting and strutting our own stuff. There is a way which seems right in the eyes of men but the end is the way of death. We must ever be careful of false labels, we could be swallowing deadly poison and not realize it.

As for those who wish to call wrong right, I would like to point them to a verse of Scripture. Proverbs 17:15. *"He that justifieth the wicked, and he that condemneth the just even they both are abomination to the Lord."* Just what is this verse saying? Can we misinterpret it; I think it is highly unlikely that we can. It is so plain that a child can understand it. Many are going about doing just what the Bible condemns. Marching in the parades of the wicked and endorsing their evil deeds unware of their own condemnations, yet purporting to be in the camp of the just. These are the same people who cringe at the thought or the sight of a righteous person in the public arena standing up for Godliness and morality.

These people might not themselves be reprobate, that is hardened sinners but they are nevertheless condemned by God; notwithstanding their respectable appearances. They are off the narrow path and are on the path that leads to destruction.

Living righteously tops the chart of purposeful living. We are on top of the world when we live subliminally. Of course, we do not get to the pinnacle of our game overnight, it takes time and 60 practice. I believe just as the athlete strengthens his endurance and strength by practice and exercise, so we too must make it our duty to indulge in the Word and have close fellowship with our Father. Keep engaged in the community of believers and enjoy the secure life.

Are there believers and "True" believers?

To attach "true" to a believer is to suggest that there are more than one category of believers. In all of life there are degrees of comparison. Things are graded according to quality but in the realm of Christianity it is not so. There is but one believer, not a believer and a true believer and so on. You are either in or you are out of the kingdom. Many times I witness to someone and then I will ask them if they are saved and they would say they hope so. That leads me to ask another direct question. "Are you married?" Now they dare not say I hope so. They know if they are married or not and can give a definitive answer.

Since there is a criterion for entering the Kingdom of God we can know and in fact we must know whether we are in or not. Christ specifically sets it out that we must be born again. We must receive the new birth to become a Christian. So then, the Christian is a born again person.

There is only one Church, one body of believers, one congregation of saints, one baptism, one repentance, one of all these because there is only one Saviour. There are no degrees of salvation. You have received Christ as your Lord and Saviour or you have rejected Him. His commandments are His words. Our own thoughts on any matter cannot supersede His Words. It is folly to think otherwise. Jesus said: *"...Except a man be born again he cannot see the kingdom of God."* John 3:3. Have you ever wanted to get into something so badly you would do anything legally to gain admittance? It is something that is advertised perhaps: A new car, a new motorcycle, a new suit or so forth. You can have whatever the offering is, with the exception that you make the down payment. The seller will not discriminate as long as you come up with the required down payment. Entering the Kingdom is for anyone, rich or poor as long as you submit and repent. Submitting to Christ is the only purposeful living there is.

CHAPTER 8

BE NOT DECEIVED

61 Deception in our day and indeed throughout the history of man is as widespread as the sky above us. It envelopes all of society, everywhere man dwells and in spite of its universality we still succumb to its pull. We get sucked in because inherent in the character of man is the compass of trust. There is the truth principle and we know deep down that we can trust someone. Therein lay our downfall when we put our trust in the wrong thing or the wrong person. Since deception is so widespread, we have to walk gingerly through life, not placing implicit trust in anyone but God Himself. God alone is absolutely trustworthy and His every word can be trusted and must be relied upon as truth. Every word of man we must view as suspect and taken with a grain of salt. When we realize that this is the condition of our world, then are we ready to live wisely.

The most singular of all events took place at Calvary, Two Thousand years ago and some do not yet know and others who know think about it less and less. This event to the world at large is fading in the background even as they rush toward a cataclysmic event. The very event that will determine their everlasting destiny they have no interest in. Some are busy buying futures and speculating for tomorrow's gain indeed but the eminent culmination of all events are on the horizon and they care not to hear about it. We are people of prodigious stupidity. We accentuate the trivial and trivialize the essentials. Look out, for things will not continue as they were from the beginning but they will not listen nor take heed. The calamity will come in like "Noah's Flood" and sweep them all away. They will know then but it will be too late to heed the warning. We have not learned to trust the trustworthy God as we should.

We look to our leaders for guidance but they themselves are lost, they are floundering and will move on into oblivion themselves because the source of blessings they know not. They are looking for wisdom, satisfaction and happiness but in the wrong places. Everyman thinks he has just the right product and the right philosophy for our plight but they are wrong. God alone has and offers the prescription for our maladies. The trouble is will we fill that prescription?

It does not matter how one comes shouting, screaming, frothing at the mouth and squinting, all of that will not detract from the veracity of the Word of God which is the standard by which we will live and prosper and die and be judged. Lay aside the Word and device other methods to live by and you falter and sink. The Philosopher Havel said: *"The Gospels is a constellation of Truths and the tragedy of modern man is not that he knows less and less about the meaning of his own life but that it bothers him less and less."* Many of us cease even to think of our mortality, we would rather not talk about it some say. Don't think of it and it will go away? Not so though, until our consciences begin to bother us and we begin to plan for the journey ahead we are in the pickle. The danger comes when we have become comfortable in our present sphere.

62 A well-known adage is: *"Out of sight out of mind."* There is some truth to this adage in that what we can't see we often forget. To be able to see into the future and beyond the horizon takes a spiritual eye but has modern man fallen into a lethargic state

where he is blinded and cannot see any more. He has drugged himself with the cares of this world that he has become immune to rational thinking and as such cannot help himself. Take a blind man out into the country at midnight and ask him to look up and count the stars in the heavens and he will do as well looking down. It will not make any difference to him. Many are stumbling blindly today toward the end and this is a gigantic tragedy that the flood is coming and they say who cares, let it wash over us, we will not move to higher ground. Such thinking or attitudes are the Devils ploy, He is deceiving the unsuspecting.

Living in dangerous times

Many come today as ERUDITES; learned men and women, showing great scholarshipbut if they are not Biblicist they are but extirpates, rooting out and destroying that which has been planted. Their only reward will be monetary, which at best are temporary but they will have no portion with the *Ecclesia* (The called out ones) they shall have their portion with the liars and deceivers and whoremongers ultimately ending up in the lake of fire. God has spoken it.

Never mind how much letters they have behind their names, if they are not possessors of life, they will have nothing to teach. Sooner or later they will be found out. Many are busy philosophising and writing their own paradigm and know little of the word of God. Saint Augustine wrote: *"It takes a truly educated mind to believe the miracles of Christ while refusing to believe in Christ."* Is this not a sad commentary? Some in Christ's day witnessed the miracles and attributed them to the devil as the source of His power. How very damning for them is that assertion. Too many are willfully ignorant of the word of God and the dictates of God Himself. They perish amidst a sea of information pointing to their future.

In Matthew 12: 22-24: "Then was brought unto Him one possessed with a devil, blind and dumb: and He healed him. 23 And all the people were amazed and said, is not this the son of David?

24 But when the Pharisees heard it they said, this fellow doth not cast out devils, but by Beelzebub the prince of the devils." And the people were amazed at the miracle; that is the ordinary people but not the educated folks. They were the spin doctors and had to attribute the miracle disparagingly; to the Devil. He could not be credited for who He said He was because they knew His father and mother and his sisters and brothers. Are these the people who we should listen to who dispense lies and not the truth? They come with fancy words but lack

63 trustworthiness. There is no greater force than the truth. All of us are in bondage and it is the truth and nothing but the truth that will set us free.

This next statement may seem like a diatribe and it is because what I write about is truth and when I hear men speaking of things they know little or nothing of it irks me. In essence the Lord needs no defence but I cannot go undisturbed by their baseless and outlandishpostulations. Many speak from what they assume things to be and not what they truly are because they have no base for their words. They do not read the word and be taught by it. They deal with God's business as though they were selling an ordinary product and any ingenuity will help push that product. Some have no conscience at all, they will lie blatantly even from the pulpit. God help us to be honest men and women discerning the signs of the times and dispensing the truth. I am distressed by some of the things they site as coming from the throne of God. Men and women coming to us as though they were sent especially from God to give us something new and we swallow much of it. We would better know what's written in the Scriptures or else we will swallow their lies. Whether the falsehood is deliberate or not, we must know our Bible so we can discern falsehood when it appears. God help us to be discerning and discriminating men and women. We are commanded to study the Word for that same reason. Here I have examples of two men whom I have encountered who come as learned men of God and some of the things they said are of their own opinions only and are not Biblical. The first man I encountered at the Seminary who came at the invitation of the Professor to give us atalk on his Christian faith. We had the opportunity to ask question after the discourse. One of my questions to him was: "Do you believe that Mary was a perpetual virgin." His answer was:

"Which young woman would bear the Lord Jesus Christ and go on to have more children?" In his opinion that would not be considered. Now let us look at the Scriptures and see whether Mary had more children or not.

In the Gospel of Mark 6:33 Jesus' family was named by the skeptics after Jesus preached in the synagogue in the preceding verse. It reads: "Is not this the carpenter, the son of Mary, the brother of James and Joses and Judah, and Simon? And are not his sisters here with us? And they were offended at Him." Needless to say this man has never read as far as this portion of Scripture which delineated Jesus' family. How can we hear them if they bear not the truth?

64 The second man more recently spoke at a church and he spoke of something very contrary to the word and teachings of Jesus Christ. He said to us that Jesus was praying for the seven billion inhabitants here on earth. That sounds like a likely thing to do; Jesus praying for all the

Inhabitants of earth and the logical conclusion of this prayer is that every person on earth would then be saved for the Father honours the son's prayers. We know that that is not so and the Bible teaches otherwise. Let us examine John 17:9. "I pray for them: [those who are saved] I pray not for the world but for them which thou hast given me; for they are thine." These are Jesus' words versus man's. A Christian must bear the testimony of his

Lord, Jesus Christ; we are nothing more than messengers, and ambassadors.

We cannot contradict God's word to interject our own opinions, that is diabolical and one should not claim to be teachers of the Word when they are ignorant of it. The Apostles spoke with conviction of the things which they had seen and heard and knew to be true not on speculative opinions. They spoke of facts not fiction. In life, we tend to embellish the truth somewhat at times but to invent the truth is another matter altogether. Many are inventing some truths to be popular, it cannot be done.

Many today are trying to work the works of God; it cannot be done. All that is needed is to present the truth, the Gospel of Christ. In Jesus' day they asked Him the same question. "… what shall we do that we might work the works of God? John 6:28. Jesus answered and said unto them, this is the work of God that ye believe on him whom he hath sent." To believe that Jesus is the Christ, the son of the living God is the faith that we need to exercise and nothing more. Having believed this fact ends the struggles in our lives and we can rest in the assurance that we have eternal life at this juncture. This simple faith gives us a foothold on eternal life and then we can begin to practice our faith by plunging into deeper truths of His word.

Belief or faith is not based on speculations or opinions but on the written Word of God. Christians embrace as truth what is written in the Scriptures without wavering. Our eternity depends upon it, pure and simple. Yes! we are where we set out to be when we trust the Word of God. We are in His Kingdom; it is left to us now to enjoy the blessings and privileges of the Kingdom. May God help us to discern and use these privileges to the maximum?

I would like to warn you readers that there are many false prophets out their vying for your eternal souls. Be careful what you hear and swallow, please check things out for yourselves. The stake is too high for you to gamble with it. We have heard of noblemen and indeed we consider them to be great men of wealth and of high birth but we too can be listed as noble

65 when we are diligent searchers of truth. The Book of Acts of the Apostles states in 17:11. *"These were more noble than those in Thessanolica, in that they received the word in all readiness of mind and searched the scriptures daily, whether those things were so."*

In today's world with information at our fingertips no one should be ignorant about eternal truths. We should not stumble in the dark and fall into the abyss as those whose eyes remain blinded will do eventually. We all have a responsibility and we are going to be held accountable for our actions. We will not be able to say I did not know as an excuse. We seek to clarify other things but the things of eternal value we neglect, how can that be. We will perish with the ignorant as though there was never a warning given. A person would declare that after sixty or seventy years there is only one person who had ever approached him with the Gospel. Has he not heard the programs on TV and radios and seen the dozens of churches around him?

Let us awaken therefore and live. Let us hear the whole council of God and not man's. It is a fearful thing to fall in the Hands of an angry God. It is prudent to say the least to fall at His feet and humble ourselves and get his approbation instead of men's. The truth is borne out time and time again in living proof, as we see men fall in desperation at the foot of the Cross before their departure from this life, even after they had spent a lifetime fighting against God and writing their own prescription for life's solution instead of following God's. In the end they have seen the light and it enlightened them and brought them out of darkness into His eternal light.

CHAPTER 9

EMBOLDEN BY PRIDE

There is sadness in the lives of men where there should be happiness and gladness instead. Here I am reminded of one such man, Friedrich Nietzsche, a German philosopher, a man who some consider the most-influential philosopher of all modern thinkers. He is considered influential because he purports a new paradigm, one which deviates from the path of godliness and morality. In essence he reasoned that we should find a new mode of thinking. It was another German who reminded us at the University that the basis of knowledge comes from the Bible and that without its knowledge one was not fully educated. Every Christian can endorse this statement as true. This professor has embraced the Bible as truth and as the basis of his knowledge and he is living and enjoying life to its fullest. He was not ashamed to publicly state this fact to his class. When the truth reigns, it emboldens a person and that is the power of His word.

66 Those who are so wise that they think that they can jump over God and His truth are but fools themselves. It is time that will bear out the truth as In the case of Nietzsche who was terrorized by his own conscience before his death. It is well to be reminded that there is the law of sowing and reaping. *"Whatsoever a man soweth that shall he also reap."* Galatians 6:7.

A man who wonders out of the path of truth then must reside in the congregation of the dead. It is a law that we will succumb to every time. A man will reap what he sows. Sow to the wind and you will reap a whirlwind but sow in love and humility and you will reap a harvest of sweet fruits. A life of rest and peace awaits the humble and the penitent soul.

Imagine four men sitting at a table discussing the future of the world as men do occasionally. They are men from the four corners of thought. The one at the head of the table is a Communist, the other opposite to him is Darwin, right of the Communist is an Agnostic and opposite him is a Christian. They have been at their discussion for quite some time now and have not been able to make a dent into each other's thinking. Each man holding firm to his belief, of course because each is fully convinced that he is right and as such there is no need to relent. After all, each is deeply entrenched in his beliefs and way of life and that strangeness would engulf them if he should even think of changing. As they togged to and fro in their discussion on what is true, they were interrupted by this frightful noise of this distinguished looking gentleman, Nietzsche: God is dead, God is dead, God is dead he declared rather boisterously.

They did their best to quieten him down and after some time they invited him to take a seat. So added to the table of four is this most distinguished figure Frederick Nietzsche. He is busy but surely he can spare a few minutes to talk about this important matter for a little. He decides to sit and have a discussion. With news of such tremendous importance everyone wants to know the source of the news. A man needs clarification of the news of such gigantic proportion and surely one should spare the time to alley any doubt by listening to the bearer of such news.

The Communist was a Russian and the first to speak. "So Friedrich I do not know where you got this news from because I have been searching all over for God and I know He doesn't exist except in the minds of men and women. I have searched for Him even in space and He was not there. This God you speak of is only a figment of your imagination. He simply does not exist. You cannot convince me that you saw a dead God."

"Well" replied Friedrich: You might have a point there that He might have been only an imagination. Up until today, I lived with the consciousness of a being inhabiting the earth but now that thought is replaced by vagueness and emptiness. The thought has simply vanished like

67 a vapour. The interesting thing now is, I feel free and without any compunction whatsoever. I feel unnaturally free and He must be dead. Yes I declared Him dead, dead, dead."

The next to interrogate him was the Agnostic. "In all of my life" he said: I had no certainty that there was a God and today you have come to tell me that you have found the body of God. He is dead. I need closure and therefore I will accompany you to see the body myself." That request went unanswered.

Next to speak was Charles Darwin as they rotated clockwise around the table. "So Friedrich you are a very clever man, my friends Nicketa and Hansen in their lives could not find a trace of Him and suddenly you have stumbled upon His body. This day shall not pass by without me seeing and witnessing it. Frankly I knew that there is no God since we are all here by chance and everything evolved into what they are today, *Ex Nihilo*. I have proven it by my research and many brilliant minds have also confirmed my research. There really is no God but I will spare the time to look at the body. Surely there must be some truth to this; since you are the most brilliant among us here I can attest. Everyone in high places speak highly of your insight into new things. No wonder you of all people should make such a remarkable discovery."

Christian was the last to speak. "Mr. Nietzsche" he asked: "When did you get the news that God is dead. Did you stumble upon His body or did someone else tell you. If you saw Him yourself what was His condition. Was he dead when you saw Him or was he dying and drew His last breath in your presence? Was He in agony or did He die peacefully. Did He ask for anyone in particular, did He speak of a will or did He make any request as His last words? Tell us please. As a custom every time a member of one's family dies the next of kin are notified and I was not aware of this death. Can you tell me a little more so that I might understand the oversight why I was not made aware of it? Just what happened; did He have an accident or was it from old age or whatever, please let me know. Did you positively identify the body?" As a compassionate man did you ever offered to resuscitate Him? Rendered CPR, gave a drink of water or whatever. Give us the details please. Just don't stand there, let us know what happened man?"

Nietzsche was in a quandary now, it was obvious. His complexion changed and his demeanour shows an uneasiness that was not there before. Composure gives way torambling. The Russian could never have located Him although he searched the heavens with his space crafts and the Agnostic could never pin Him down either and Darwin knew for sure that He never existed and it came as a surprise that now someone has evidence of His existence. The Christian who knew that He exists wants to see the body but only sarcastically. He demands the *Habeas Corpus*. Then and only then will he and the rest of the family have closure.

68 Nietzsche was cornered like a caged bird; he did not know what to do and how to answer all these questions. He was simply dumbfounded, speechless as one who could not talk. His so-called brilliance came pressing down on him like a ton of bricks.

Nietzsche in announcing God's death was two Thousand years too late and if he were doing so, he would need a qualifier. He would have to announce that the son of God or God the son was dead and that was on the cross of Calvary. He would have been right then but he is forever too late to announce such an event. Christ died in effect and rose and declared Himself:*"I am He that liveth and was dead; and, behold, I am alive forevermore,*

Amen; and have the keys of hell and of death." Revelation 1:18. These are the facts and we no longer speak of a dead God but a risen Saviour.

With these pressing questions from his audience he ran out asking for more time and he got all the time he needed for his time here was cut short so that he would have more of eternity to prove his theory that God is dead. He lived a short life, barely fifty six and became as mad as a shark as he made his exit. Although a Sophist, he lived a sordid life and died as a tale that was told. He sought only vainglory as he lived and did not consider his eternal wellbeing. His god was indeed dead now and forever more for he would not again be able to lift up his eyes and say Lord have mercy. He would not hear from God again for all eternity. He had written his own obituary. 'Nietzsche, Lost'.

Christian spoke to him, spoke to them all in fact but they all went away unconvinced and resolute in their beliefs as they had gathered around the table that day. The sun dries the clay and melts the butter. It has a purpose and it never fails to do its work. The Word of God releases the soul in the grip of Hell and hardens the heart of unbelief but is ever doing its work.

Christian continues to shout and declare that His God reigns and does it with every assurance and confidence like Job who knew that His redeemer liveth and He ever liveth to make intercession for us before the Father. Such great affirmation of faith by Job to be able to trust in spite of the most horrible of sufferings, confirms the truth that when we see God, self is insignificant. Job saw beyond the present suffering to a better life because of his great faith.

This very act of Job shows us that happiness depends on happenings while joy comes from knowing God. When we are connected to God through reconciliation, there can be no distraction through or because of any hardships or suffering. We have the witness in us and we know that all things work together for our good at all times and not just sometimes. We must believe that He is in charge of our lives completely. Since I believe this to be so, then when cancer knocked at my door why should I despair and call the church to pray for me when God is saying Trevor, get your house in order you are leaving this earth. This is what I intend to do and

69 nothing less. God has spoken. I have been thinking and saying, why should a person having lived to be seventy or eighty and still crying for a few more years, what for? By the time this book is published I will be eighty or closer to it or even dead, I cannot tell but I am doing as usual whatever I can until I can't do anything anymore. If I can read this sentence in the book I will be happy. Let's see.

This is the confidence that I have in the scheme of things and I fear for the one who is vacillating between this world and the next, not having the confidence that God, our Great God knows best. We must not only say that we believe in God we must believe God implicitly. Know that what He says is so. To the redeemed, His promise is to take us home to be with Him and why should not I be delighted to see His face? Now is my time and I do not want to linger here one moment longer. I once heard a Baptist preacher said we should welcome the chance to depart this life when death knocks. I said amen to that. So am I a two timer now to want to resist the opportunity. I will not resist. This is my conviction and I am sticking with it. We must settle the matter while everything is well and not wait until catastrophe strikes and then we decide what to do.

I am convinced that the greatest regret of people in Hell will be that they had heard the word and spurned it. They will be tormented by that thought day and night throughout eternity much more than the burning fire itself. It is only as we live we have the opportunity to repent. There is never another time when we will be given another chance to do so and that is not my saying but the Word of God. The Lord Jesus Christ said: "...*except ye repent ye shall all likewise perish.*" Luke 13:3. What a life I often say. How easy it is for one to submit to God's authority, pick up a passport to heaven and await you turn to board the flight. How assuring this thought is, it is incomprehensible.

Can we know the truth when we discover it? Can we recognize and assimilate that truth? Of course, we will know the truth when we have it. It is like hearing about the ocean described in its majestic splendour and might; its vastness, its strength and its warmth and wonder if you came upon such a sight if you would recognize it. Yes you would, you would not fail to recognize this enormous body of water as the ocean. You would not mistake it for a thousand deserts or a million waterfalls. This splendour and enormous force would hit you as nothing else you have seen: so is the truth of God's word when you assimilate it. God's word is the only sustaining and stabilizing force you will ever know, it is the settling peace that anyone longs ever for. God's word is the greatest force this world has ever known, it has the power to move you from earth to Heaven and who would not be thrilled about that. We are thrilled when we lift off on an airplane but the greatest thrill awaits the Christian yet.

70 The truth has a liberating grandeur and a magnificent fragrance and it has inviting warmth that envelops us and we know that we have received it when it hits us. It showers us with copious and intoxicating assurance. The truth is liberating and settles a person firmly in their sphere of influence. It makes us genuine people. It transforms us into credible beings, for the first time in our lives and others can take us at our word. You have been out and lonely and you have met a thousand aunts and uncles and hugged by them but none of that compares to meeting your long lost mother. That is the satisfying hug you have longed for. You have received that hug as the real deal, the ultimate hug. Truth is embraced in the same way.

The truth is like a bell, it rings with a clear and unambiguous sound and when there is an uncertain sound we know that there is a defect in that bell. God's truth is pure and undiluted and it is detectable. The GPS which was planted in us at creation points us eventually to homewhen we zero in on the truth. We will know that we are home when we feel relaxed and at ease in our souls. Everyone who has ever met Jesus Christ knows the transformation in their lives. They will not seek contentment elsewhere after they have found it. The Author of truth gives His approval when we embrace the truth. In other words, the Holy Spirit of God bears witness with our spirits that we have come into the "Truth" when we receive the Word of truth. The believer has that witness and knows it.

We often hear the talk about "Believers" how some who call themselves believers would describe others as "True Believers" well there are no degrees of believers. There is not the believer, then a true believer and the truest believer. There are no degrees of beliefs. You are a believer or you are not. You are in or you are out. We are termed narrow minded or bigots but the truth always hurts. There must never be anything but the truth. There are so many who would like to be included in the Kingdom on their own terms and many preachers are accommodating them also. The churches are brimming with saints and overflowing with sinners at the same time; all believing they are heading in the same direction but the truth is otherwise.

John Wesley White in his book; "Thinking the Unthinkable" states: "When I was at Oxford University, C.S. Lewis told about going to hear a certain preacher. The young man ended his sermon by suggesting: "If you do not heed these words, there will be eschatological consequences." Shaking hands with him at the church door, Lewis asked, "Did you mean that if your hearers didn't believe in Christ, they'd go to Hell." "Yes" replied the young pastor. "Then why didn't you tell them" said Lewis.

Hell is a hot topic and most preachers would like to drop it as easily as they drop a hop potato but Christ spoke thirteen times more of Hell than he spoke of Heaven. It stands to reason that if we felt that the fire of Hell is real as Christians, we would not rest for telling people, begging

71 them even to escape it. Heaven is pictured as the pleasant pastures and so forth but the more demanding aspect of the Gospel is to warn people to flee from the wrath of God by repentance so as to avoid the place call Hell. Never mind where others are going, just do not go to Hell. Just escape Hell and all will be fine. This is my personal invitation to you the reader, please heed the warning. Hell was created for the rebellious angels including the Devil himself and not humans but because of our disobedience, God says Hell has enlarged its mouth to accommodate us. By all means please avoid it by coming to Christ.

How easy it is for us to be none confrontational and hide our true self so we can walk through and mingle with the crowd and be liked as though we are one of them. When I worked for the TTC as an operator I came into the lunch room one day and saw a co-worker reading a Bible and he saluted me as brother and I told him that I could nor embrace him as a brother because he does not believe as I do. I also had to call out a professor at the University also when he called himself a believer. I told him he could not call himself a believer, after he denies so many dogmas of the Bible.

If anyone has not grasped and internalizes the essence of the message of the Bible he or she is an outcast. Christ has said if you love me you will keep my commandments. To be a part of the army of Christ or to be His disciple you will have to come clean, all or none at all. He called us to a life of commitment and denial: are we willing to pay the price. That is the question, are we willing to pay the price to follow the Lord. Too many are looking back after they have taken up the plow or the cross. Christ says in either case, you are not fit when you come half-heartedly.

I often hear some say I wished I believed as you do. I read the same Bible he reads and the declaration is the same everywhere that Christ Jesus came into the world to save sinners and I do qualify, so I am in. No one needs be without Christ and His provision for sin because it is not difficult to qualify. The smallest child qualifies and the most retched and disconsolate person does. We are all possessors of the nature which automatically qualifies us. There is no exemption and if you think otherwise there you have wondered into the path of death. The Word is for the sinner great and small; pure and simple.

In the Acts of the Apostles 24:16 Festus said to Paul when Paul witnessed to Him: *"…; much learning doth make thee mad."* Festus' reasoning was biased and the content of Paul's witness was misconstrued but we can say of Friedrich Nietzsche his little learning did make him mad. His proposition was the most preposterous of all statements and he will have all of eternity to prove the gravity of his presumption. He had a choice but he took the wrong road. Fame and popularity are greater in this life than humility to most. To be the purveyor of a new doctrine is

72 a magnificent thing and something to be lauded for. He made his mark as a brilliant mind and lost his soul to the Devil, how absurd is that. Many have played the fool too long and some are playing it right now, some who have had enough light to get up and get going. Here we can deduct from the life of Friedrich Nietzsche that he took a wrong turn and it landed him in a hot spot. His error was monumental, one from which he can never recover. Be careful dear reader for wanting to be popular and smart, it could land you in something very, very hot.

Do not miss this chance

Many then missed the opportunity to submit to Christ and many even today cannot see that He has come and are hoping and praying for another appearing. Of the seventeen million Jews worldwide, those who are true to their faith, pray each morning: *"I believe with complete faith in the coming of the Messiah; even though He tarry, yet I will wait for Him every coming day."* Did the Jews not reject Him when He came two Thousand years ago? Yes they did. Those of them or anyone for that matter who are looking for His coming will see Him not as their Messiah but as their Judge. His next appearing will be in that capacity only; as Judge. Their prayers are not being heard because they can only be heard through Jesus Christ and they reject Him.

When I was a boy, on one occasion my dad sent me to do some business and I boldly bet another boy that I had more money than he had and I lost the bet.

A fright suddenly gripped me and I held the boy in such a grip he literally could not turn. He was frightened and I was too because he was a much bigger boy than I. I simply could not lose the bet because the money was not mine. Another time my mother sent me to collect some money and there was a cycle race between two cyclist and nearing the end of the race there came a cyclist and was shouting out the leader and some men from the district of one of the cyclist or the one loosing were willing to bet two to one. When I got home and told my mother, she said to me: "Why didn't you bet some money." Well in both instances the monies were not mine and I could not afford to lose any of those monies. On the latter case, a big risk might have been the key to a great gain but the essence of the matter is, we should never risk what we cannot afford to lose. Whatever losses we suffer here in the earthly realm are trivial compared to losing our souls; that loss we literally cannot afford.

73 This is something we all possess which is of infinite worth and that is our eternal souls. We lose our health, our wealth our families and so on but the loss of one's soul is an irreversible loss. The Lord Jesus states in Mathew 16:26; that a man would not gain anything if he should gain the whole world and lose his soul. Consider the worth of a soul. It is priceless. It is eternal, it is that part of a person that lives on throughout eternity. If anyone tells you otherwise do not believe them and you don't want to test that theory. You do not want to find out that you were wrong

or misguided and sided with the wrong person. You backed the loosing horse.

Reader, if you have not known the truth about an eternal soul, then find a church and ask the minister. Give the matter your uttermost attention and have that truth under your belt without delay. You will be delighted that you did. A word to the wise is always sufficient. Nietzsche and all those so called great thinkers will not fare any better than the poor ignorant man in the most destitute condition anywhere in the darkest of places where there is no knowledge of God. The reason is; God is no respecter of persons. The soul that sinneth shall die says the Lord God Almighty and unless that soul repents and turns to Christ, Who only can give new life, the end is hopeless. Throughout the Bible, the warning is to turn from our wicked ways and repent and be saved from the wrath of God to come.

Man is bankrupt, he is in the red on the balance sheet or on the debit side of the ledger big times but he pretends otherwise and he is trying his uttermost to put a spin on things by trying to turn it into a sense of rights and entitlement. He thinks still that he has the wherewithal to pull himself out of his deficit. He is slow of learning if he thinks otherwise. It cannot be done. God has spoken and unless a person repents, he shall likewise perish. Be not deceived beloved.

CHAPTER 10

INTEGRITY AND ACCOUNTABILITY

Accountability and integrity sets the pattern and standard for our lives. We can ask the question how many men and women do you know that have standards, high standard that is. How many men and women of integrity do you know? Many would say, not many, and why is that. The reasons are many. Many of us sell our worth and trust for silver and gold. We would rather pander to the wishes of the masses than do the honourable thing which would cost us something. We would rather lie than tell the truth in order to profit financially.

I have a personal story, another of course which I must interject here. I drive a school bus and one morning after the morning run I came to park the bus. I began to back up beside

74 another and I heard a slight crash. I pulled forward and backed up again to complete the process. I came out and looked where I thought I hit the bus and saw nothing. I then believed that it was the overhanging branches that the top of the bus brushed on that caused the sound.

Well I was happy or delighted that that was so. In the evening when I came back to park, I noticed broken lenses on the ground then I realized that I must have hit by bus on the other. When I examined the back lenses there it was, one broken and another cracked. Things started to enter my mind. Should I report it and lose a bonus of seven hundred and fifty dollars or say someone broke it overnight. We experience vandalism all the time so that would be accepted.

Something much larger loomed into my mind. Would I sell my Saviour for seven hundred and fifty dollars and the answer was no. I would not barter for my life if it came to that, I am sure. So if I would give my life for the cause of Christ why would I sell Him now for so small a price? I settled the question and the next morning after the run I went to the shop to report it and have it repaired. When I drove in, I saw the foreman and told him to look after it for me while I go upstairs and complete the paper work. He said don't worry I will look after it and if no one yet knows about it let it rest there. He called a mechanic and told him to take care of it and that was that. This man I saw but once before so he was not a friend but he was there to set things right for me when I needed him. You be the judge as to whether I should resist him and report it. Think of what you would do and set me free or condemn me. I did collect my seven hundred and fifty dollar bonus and I was happy to get it. The records did not show an accident for the period.

I do not want to write about something that I know nothing of. The things I write are my personal experiences, whether they are secular or spiritual. Many of us say we belong to the Christian faith and are as superficial as the shallow soil and cannot bear fruit. We gamble with our souls and risk losing all. Were we like the firemen, dedicated, committed and completely sold out to duty, our world would know wrong from right? We would know what integrity, accountability and commitment are. Those men have leaders and in their sphere of work the leaders are called Captains. The captains make the calls and that is without question even if it seems like a suicide mission.

Our most memorable disaster, tragedy or terrorism occurred in New York in the year 2000 and we forever know it as 9/11.

That date is itched in our memory those of us who were alive then as the most heinous act of non-aggression the human race has ever seen. It reveals commitment albeit misguided commitment and dedication to the point where men would give up their lives to the destruction of others. On the other hand there are men who are in high

75 places given the responsibility to work for the Master of the vineyard and stumble with the willingness to perform truthfully.

The day of 9/11, my cousin Levon Neil was in one of the "Twin Towers" and when he was coming out and saw these firemen ascending the stairs, he said he told these undaunted men that they could not go into that inferno, but they ignored their pleas and replied: "It is our job, It is our job." It is our job, meaning our lives are not ours; we have given it to the protection and saving of other lives, our lives are of no consequence as firemen. We know what happened to them, a complete contingent was wiped out. They were recognized as "firefighters" going in but they never came out except as ashes, unrecognizable.

Would politicians, ministers of the Gospel and men and women in positions of trusts live and be willing to die that way. Would be that the two pillars of our lives, integrity and accountability reign supremely in our lives.

Samuel Johnson once said: *"There can be no friendship without confidence and there can be no confidence without integrity." Integrity* is integral or essential to any life, be it an ordinary person or one in a position of trust. To be trustworthy is an honourable accomplishment; it is worth all the tea in China. It is a crown you can wear like no other in this sin-cursed earth.

In the year 2015 I spent some time in Jamaica on the mission field in the area where I grew up. I covered a large area on foot, witnessing, taking pictures and giving out tracts. One man told me that the man whom his wife worked for as a domestic help told him that he has known me for a long time and whatever I told him to do he can do it. I knew this man from my first job with the Bauxite Company. As a matter fact I met this brother (for now he had become a Christian since we worked together) at a Moravian Church I visited while on that trip.

The word integrity implies: Moral uprightness; honesty; wholeness; rectitude; completeness; soundness; unimpaired or uncorrupted condition. Such are the words that describe a person of integrity. He or she is indefatigable: cannot be worn out, unwavering and unremitting. He cannot be bought or sold. He stands as the rock of Gibraltar, unmovable. We must endeavour to live as such a person. Colonel Robert E. Lee of the Confederate army during the civil war in the United States after his surrender was offered an opportunity to make some money, a lucrative amount but he turned it down. It was to use his name to promote a certain product. His reply: "All I have left is my reputation." Further to that he said: "…be an accumulation of all the evils we complain of, and I am willing to sacrifice everything but honour for its preservation." I would not waste a page to tell you of the many times I have been conned by men bearing the badge of Christianity and yet such honourable men abound in the secular world. Unsaved they are but honourable nevertheless.

76 Sometimes we fall into situations as Christians and we are willing to compromise and we reason that we will be forgiven for compromising but on the broader picture if we compromise on small issues we will not be able like the firemen to die for our cause. We would better be in practice so why not start now.

Come to think of it, were these firemen confronted with the thought that they might sacrifice their lives on the morning of 9/11 or were they facing such situation every morning when they go out to work? I believe they face that possibility every morning and knew and resigned themselves to the idea that such might be the case where they would have to put their lives on the line. The disaster did not build their resolve it only tested it. There is always an acid test in our lives and the question is, will we be able to pass that test? Every adversity builds or weakens our character. Your response to a situation depends upon your character. Especially as Christians, we need to build good characters.

I spoke with a man recently who told me of a situation which he ran into. He saw a car advertised and phoned in to the seller who told him that the car was promised already to someone else. However, after speaking for some time with this man; this prospective purchaser said: "Why don't you take my number just in case." Well the just in case happened and the prospective purchaser received a call. He went and when he saw the car, he offered the seller more than he advertised it for. The seller proclaimed that he did not want one penny more than he spent to have the car brought up to standard. He could not be persuaded otherwise for he said: "I am a Christian." He is a man of integrity. He exhibits soundness of character. There was simply no wavering on his commitment to deliver. Would we all be as prudent in our dealings as this man was? A great sermon was preached that day by this Christian whom I am sure had a more lasting effect than many preached from decorated pulpits.

In John 1:47: Jesus saw Nathanael coming to Him and said of him: *"Behold an Israelite indeed, in whom is no guile!"* What would Jesus be saying to many of us if He saw us coming. I believe many of us would not be coming to Him but running away from Him because of our state.

We mentioned a little earlier that if we build our lives on the two pillars of accountability and integrity we would now have something to sustain us in the swelling of Jordon. Unless we build such a life we will not have the sustenance in the swelling of Jordon. Are we then building for time or for eternity? This is the broader question we must ask ourselves as we make our way through life, as we sojourn down here on earth. Are we building lives that will survive the fire of scrutiny by our Maker? He is the One we are ultimately accountable to. If we bear that in mind that He is our Captain like the Firemen in 911, we shall do well.

A Self-made Person

77 We hear so often of the self-made person and our eyes pop out and our attention sharpen at such terms but we are all self-made to a certain extent. We are all Builders or Architects if you will, building in this wall of time some with massive deeds and great, some with ornaments of rhyme. Whose lives are we building in essence? Our lives, individual lives that are stacking up to buttress our existence or to act as a load and will flatten us. We must act so that each tomorrow finds us further than today. Each today strengthens our drive to get in the fray again tomorrow to fight and to win. Each successive day and its successes spur us on to greater heights. Living with this attitude is a must for a successful life. A victorious life and an overcoming one is conducive not only to our wellbeing but to those round about us as well.

Investment is the single most important thing that we hear in the world today especially in the business world. Investment, we are encouraged to invest our monies in some fund or bond or stock, but we are encouraged to invest. When I go to fill up my tank at the gas station I am encouraged to invest in some *lotto* ticket at the checkout counter. I cheerfully respond with a smile and a word: *"I win every day because I keep my money."* I have noticed large sums being leafed out to buy Lotto tickets and that is with the hope of winning. How sad. I see some are on their last lap and yet I wonder if they won, what improvements would they make to their lives. Not much I believe. Some lives are at the edge of the grave and instead of planning for the next life they are here hanging unto this fleeting one. I will still say: How sad. How sad that that is all there is to many.

All of life is perception. How does one view their life here on earth? Do they see it as an endless existence destined to go on for ever and forever and as such they do not know when to slow down or even to rest? Do they not read the history of mankind and see the end of all men. Have they not visited the graveyard sometimes? When I witnessed to a man in Jamaica he said to me: "Don't tell me about death, tell me about life." If one is not willing to entertain the reality of death, then he is deceiving himself. He is simple suspending the inevitable. There are two appointments that we dare not miss: Death and the Judgement.

King David in Psalm 144: 3-4 States: *"Lord, what is man, that thou takest knowledge of him? Man is like to vanity: his days are as a shadow that passeth away."* When and if we get a hold on what is said here, our attitude about life is bound to change? It must change both to ourselves and toward others. If we fathom the gravity of those words then our hold on possessions should not be as rigid as some of us hold them. We would grasp things lightly and not let them drag us into a life of degradation and ruin. We must live our lives therefore as we perceive things. It is forever, so we hold fast or it is fleeting so we hold lightly.

78 The most single investment we can make in life is in ourselves, that is; keeping a proper balance of our four dimensions: The physical, the spiritual, the social and the mental. When we keep these in balance we are beginning to see the real value of life and can grow in the stature we are intended to become and will be in a position to assist others with their difficulties as well. Self is the only instrument we have to deal with life and with others and as such we must keep it healthy and well balanced. We must keep that equilibrium to be effective in living or navigating the shark infested waters. We are the instruments of our own performance and we must take time to tune that instrument. Develop a prayer life as Christians, memorize Scriptures which is a daily reading of God's word, eat healthy foods and exercise regularly. Keep the mental and physical, social and spiritual well balanced and life will be a breeze. It will not be burdensome as you journey through it. You will find more pleasant pastures in which to dwell than not.

We have seen those people who appear as though they are living on top of everything andunlike Charles Atlas; their world is not on their shoulders. Many have come to carry the burdens of the world on their shoulders sadly enough. There is one who is responsible to carry that weight and it is not a human being. It is the responsibility of the Great Creator Himself and I personally think it is His job so I leave it with Him. Our primary responsibility is to ourselves first and then to those round about us. We sustain our wellbeing and in so doing we are most effective in helping others. A well sustained and balanced life is like a balanced budget. Things run smoother when a budget is balanced in a household or anywhere else for that matter. Life in essence becomes less complex and runs on less energy. It becomes a simpler and manageable proposition. We live simply with less stress. Stress as we know is deadly; it is living with an unnecessary load on one's shoulder. The faster we manage to unload that burden or load, the more meaningful life becomes. There is an ease going through life with a light load or even none at all if that's possible.

Living with a spiritual dimension is the key to a happy life. The spiritual dimension is simply casting our cares upon the One who cares for us and can carry our load. The spiritual dimension develops the heart which in turn oils the whole body and enables it to function more easily. It allows it to run as a well-oiled machine. Develop the heart and the body will be whole. It is the source of power. It is the connection to the source of power in essence. Our hearts are what connect us to the things we love. The heart pants after the things it longs for. It seeks those things with every effort imagined. It is a longing and a hungering that besets the person and there is no rest until that thirst is quenched. Seek therefore, after the eternal things, find what they are and delight yourself in them.

79 David says in Psalm 42: 1 *"As the hart panteth after the water brooks, so panteth my soul after thee, O God."* The hart is drawn inextricably toward the water brook for it is thirsty; it knows that that is the only remedy for a searing thirst. It cannot rest; it

cannot lie down until that thirst is quenched. Would to God every Christian would express himself in like manner. That we will not rest until we have been filled with the peace and righteousness of God Himself.

Many so called Christians do not have that longing, even after a life of naming the name of Christ. They abandoned the truth of God's word in place of their own intellect. We spoke of the importance of integrity and accountability in one's life for anything lasting to come of it. Integrity is integral to any Christian's life or anyone's life for that matter but to the Christian, it is paramount. We have a command from our Leader to give all, our absolute best that is. It is like the firemen we discussed earlier. They gave their lives for the cause. We are in essence ofmore value than they are in the scheme of things for we are in the business of rescuing souls. Our lives have an eternal thrust. It is the approbation we seek at the end of the journey. "A *well done, instead of depart.*"

An important matter to consider is that Christians are just a family, that is; we affect every member of that family when we err in our conduct. We should endeavour to perpetuate the term "*Esprit de corps.*" Simply, a regard for the honour and interest of the group to which one belongs. Joshua expressed himself clearly amidst the uproar and disbelief on their journey through the wilderness to the Promised Land. He declared; *"As for me and my house we will trust the Lord."* Every Christian should echo the same sentiment. We should not be striving for wealth and security outside the Lord Jesus Christ. The anxiety should be settled and we must exhibit that security in our everyday lives. We should or must not betray our faith in a wholly trustworthy God. Many of us are as nervous about our future as the rest of the ungodly world. Shame on us I dare say.

There are many living and operating under the guise of Christianity that if it were a graded matter would still be in kindergarten according to their knowledge of truth. They have simply not grown in faith and in the knowledge of the word. Knowledge is power and to know the greatest of all events both past and future is more than comforting to any soul.

I reiterate the need to know, every chance I get so that you know that the responsibility is yours to look after your future. Do not leave it to someone else. No one can intercede or plead on your behalf. You must go to God in Jesus' name yourself. Now are we priest and Kings unto God after the cross. We all have equal standing before God. No matter what name they are called by, they have no more standing than you the repentant sinner. The many letters to or after their names do not make them more eligible than the rest of us are in seeking and

80 communicating with our Father. We are all equal in his eyes and as such, can appear boldly before the throne of God with our petitions. The least of us, God is no less our Father and will hear us as promptly as he hears the most distinguished of his servants. Sometimes this standing before God is hard to fathom but it is God's word which enlightens us to this fact and we must believe it.

It is established in God's word that He is no respecter of persons; nevertheless, not because we all have the same standing before God, that we are not to be respectful of those in Pastoral authority and other positions of the Church. Every well run family has a structure and a hierarchy. Everyone is not all cooks.

CHAPTER 11

DIFFERENT APPROACHES SAME RESULTS

We have witnessed planes coming in from all directions to land at the airports and some fromthe opposite directions from where they originated. For instance, planes coming in from the US should come in from the south and yet we see them coming in from the north. It depends upon how the wind is blowing. The planes that are landing look for a headwind and not a tail wind. As a result, regardless of the direction they are coming from they must follow the rule of the direction of the wind. Landing in the wind adds resistance to the craft and enables it to stop faster whereas a tail wind pushes the craft preventing it from stopping as quickly as possible.

This analogy is being used to illustrate the following which I want you to pay careful attention to as your future could depend on it. Consider that seemingly simple rule developed by the aviation school as a built in mechanism to provide maximum or added safety to the craft when landing. The neglect to observe this rule might or might not have dire consequences when landing but it helps as a safety feature and is used as a rule routinely. We have noticed as the title of this chapter suggests, that in case of landing a craft the directions varies considerably, landing is dictated by the prevailing wind and of necessity sometimes the rules can be brokenand as long as the craft settles safely on the tarmac; the mission is accomplished. That truly is the bottom line, the safety of the passengers. Now, there is a far weightier matter that concerns us and some of us do think that all roads lead to heaven. Like the old adage: *All road leads to Rome.* Some who are in the camp of the godly believes that also, that it does not matter what they believe as long as they are sincere. God will look upon them favourably they reason, when the day of reckoning comes. Others think as long as you keep the golden rule you will be fine and God will be pleased. Some believe that your due diligence is to go to the house of God and put some money in the offering plate and He (the Lord) will be happy and receive you on that faithful day. All of these perceptions and more are men's ideas about God and the

81 eans of gaining His favour. This aforementioned category encompasses the laypeople; the uninformed if you will but sadder still are those within the body of Christ who seek to do their own things. They make the sacrifice of Cain and their sacrifices and they will be rejected.

This second category is those who are literally making contracts without the authority of the Lord Himself. They proclaim a social doctrine to their congregation one which soothes the mind and does nothing to stir the soul. They spout from the mouth things that are contrary to Scriptures and are nevertheless satisfied with themselves at the end of the sermons. The sermons are not intended to stir the soul and to spur the congregation to soul searching and repentance but only to pacify and sometimes justify some wrongs.

Such behaviours are ridiculous to say the least and are presumptuous at its highest. God has given His servants a Word and His word is His bond. Our self-efforts are but worthless rags in His sight. None has the authority to change one dot or tittle of His word and if they do, they do so at their own peril. Some are proud and will not humble themselves under the mighty hand of God now but eventually they will have to submit. When the roll call comes they will have no leg to stand on. They will have to bow and confess that He is Lord and ruler over all. He has declared that His word cannot be voided. He swears by His word and we would better tremble at that word. *He declares that the soul that sinneth shall surely die.* Ezekiel 18:4. Psalm 119: 89 declares: *"For ever, O Lord, thy word is settled in heaven."*

Different approaches and same results refer not only to the plane landing on an airfield but to many of us. There are many who unashamedly denounce Him as none existent and many acknowledge His presence and power but are casual about His authority. Regardless of man's reasoning the Lord's authority diminishes by zero. Man might think himself worthy of notice but in God's eyes without His mercies we are absolute nothing. It is only after we are engrafted into the vine that we will amount to something. Other than that, we remain dead and impotent.

In light of eternity and God, we are all accountants. We live and maintain a certain degree of decorum in every aspect of life. There are responsibilities at every level of life and

82 accountability to someone. We cannot escape it. Those who reject that norm are languishing in the prison houses of the lands but even there, there are rules which they must obey and follow.

No one is an island to himself, we are all interconnected and are responsible to each other and the broader picture must include God in our lives for that life to be of any worth. For nothing can be fully understood without reference to God and His supreme authority. That acknowledgement is the beginning of wisdom. The sooner they get that fact into their heads the sooner they begin to walk on the high road which is the secure path. This realization is their first measure of security in this life and the one to come.

When I was a teenager our school went to play cricket against another school and we lost the match and I displayed a very bad attitude and the headmaster of that school told me something I have not forgotten since. He said to me; *"Even in Hell there are rules."* That one statement straightened me out for good. I went away nursing my wound and it still hurts even today. Every situation in life will bring some benefit no matter how insignificant it is. If we are sensitive and willing to look for opportunities and acknowledge our guilt then there is hope for us. If there exists an element of inquisitiveness still in us, then we will prevail and triumph over every circumstance providing God is in the mix.

Different approaches to God are contrary to the normal operation of businesses and will notbring the intended results. Many do think and worship as they please and believe that the slightest wind of doctrine directed toward God will be sufficient to gain them access into heaven. That God is the great magnet and every prayer and form of worship that is thrown out there will be picked up by Him is a fallacy. That He will be too happy to pick up every prayer no matter how vaguely presented it is to Him, is only wishful thinking. There is a correct name by which we address the Almighty God and an avenue by which we can approach Him. We cannot come in as the planes do on any runway. We have to approach His throne in the name of His son Jesus Christ. A prayer is of no value if it is not directed to God, the Almighty God with reverence and in the name of the Lord Jesus Christ. It is not until we recognize our unworthiness and his Omniscience that we can begin to communicate with Him. Then and only then are we in a right attitude and position to address Him as Father. To many, that realization is slow in coming and that position might never be taken but to those who see themselves as Isaiah saw himself, unworthy, then there is hope. God receives the contrite heart and the repentant person always and every time.

Different approaches and same results yes but never with God. Access is restricted to one way and only through one door and one door only and that door is clearly marked and if you

83 miss it you are off into oblivion. That door is: "Jesus Christ" We must approach God through His name or we have prayed in vain.

CHAPTER 12

BE ANXIOUS FOR NOTHING

Anxiety is a consuming passion that envelops the nations of the world and individuals alike today more so than at any other time in our history. We crave for more and more and more. Every child must possess all the toys and gadgets available in the stores and the parents must ownthe latest fashions and paraphernalia and automobiles, snowmobiles, cottage, houses, stocks and bonds, and the list is endless. With so many things to worry about, one can have no rest and time for reflection. One is simply harassing one's self to satisfy a longing an urge and sometimes only just a curiosity which subsides quickly and the rapacious person is left with a bitter taste their mouth.

My experience tells me that if you do not know where you are going or want to go then you might get there and not know it. We overrun our objectives, expending unnecessary energies quite often when we have no destination or objectives. A friend once said to me: "Many ships are docked at the harbour laden but the owners do not know and do not go to claim their goods." Is this statement a common occurrence with us, I believe so.

Jesus saw the grasping nature of men and warned them not to be anxiousbut that their heavenly father who knows all our needs will supply them in due time. Jesus Himself said: "Sufficient unto the day is the evil thereof." Let todays problem be todays problem and we deal with them today and not worry about tomorrow. In many cases this cannot be carried out to its limit, there are instances where indeed we must project ourselves and our activities into the future bur more things are provided for then, than is necessary. We make sacrifice today to meet tomorrow's needs and most times it will be unnecessary. Many times we reach old age wealthier than we had ever expected or it might not come at all. I have seen so much of it, young men and women dying prematurely, some from sheer stress. They are worrying about not having enough for tomorrow. A person under the control of the Spirit of God is a contented person and is satisfied with little which is great gain.

We are being hassle dazzled by every manufacturer's goods and are being bombarded by their ads. Some are so ridiculous it is laughable. A car manufacturer comes on TV and announces their new car as being new and improved, built for drivers. Who else do they build them for and if it is new how can it be improved. They throw out words knowing that we are suckers and will fall for anything and that we are itching for something new always. We must have it, we must have it, we are restless without it.

84 Nonsense I say. If what you have works well, then ignore the plea of the advertisers and go and rest in peace.

I have heard a granddaughter states that she wears her grandmother's clothes. That is not to say she does not buy something new for herself but she wants to show that if something is good and useable then why not use it to its fullest. I am not quick to go out and spend either, when what I have works satisfactory. I am not a Scrooge, only frugal.

The world rushers on without me and many like me I am sure. We do not have to build our own. There are many comfortable places here to dwell in peace and safety and as such we do not have to exhaust ourselves to build a new one. In the process of building, many have exhausted themselves and have exited their abode in an untimely fashion. In the midst of their thrust to remake this earth, some have been literally left behind in a box or a wheelchair. Will someone be saying this of me, probably so but believe me, if I am now talking from the grave I have embraced the things I preached on these pages. I have made right with my God and have eternity in view. I have not been inattentive to the things of eternity nor have I not lived with my mortality in front of me. If these words are read long after I am gone, know that where I am is where the Lord Jesus Christ promised I would be when I trusted in Him.

In Dubai there is such a longing for housing and craving to own and amass wealth that they are building islands to build houses on and the speculators cannot rent them because there are no renters. Those who need new housing cannot pay the exorbitant rent, therefore they remain locked up. In China there are millions of apartments and housing units that remain unoccupied for the same reasons. It is a deep seated urge that a person has for things.

Recently I was asked by a friend at the gym whether I slept well at nights and I said yes, on the contrary he said he cannot have a good night's sleep. I said to him it is a terrible thing to be rich because you stay awake worrying about your investment but if you have none then that part of one's life is settled. I am learning to live free and I am getting better at it the older I get. If all I have are my clothes at death then I shall die a comfortable death. As I revise or edit this portion which60 was already written, I realize that my time now is short, how short I don't not know but I have been given notice as I told you earlier. This notice of departure makes me a more sensible Stuart with my goods.

Conspicuous Consumption

Conspicuous consumption is the hallmark of our present society. We must show that we are affluent whether or not we really are. A copious showing is a must so as to render ourselves relevant in a society of plenty. We pretend to be what we are not and too often the price we pay which was already discussed is a high one which we need not pay.

85 The happiness of our lives flows from the quality of our thoughts. We are not who we think we are, we are simply what we think. The sum total of our lives is our thought life. Wholesome thoughts produce pure living and on the contrary corrupt and pessimistic thoughts produce a stifled and an unprofitable life. We are what we think as in we are what we eat. If we eat junk food our bodies will be malnourished, consequently if we deprive ourselves of enlivening thoughts and pollute our minds with worthless ideas and unhealthy thoughts our minds will starve and wither as well. In summation, we will be deprived mentally and produce little or no fruits. As Christians we are to produce and bear fruits always. A tree laden with fruits is a marvel to behold and the tree does not turn and eat those fruits, it is produced for the benefit of others. The beauty that is in us must be seen by others for their benefit as well. The world which is a dark place needs us as Christians to shine and be a light to them. Let us be at our post always; always performing at our best, we are needed.

We grasp after things and power but just how much enough for some people is. How much of what we need to live comfortably do we have now? Have we taken a stock recently? Look around and see if you are not where you want to be and sometimes you have far surpassed your expectations. You might be in a comfortable position right now and do not need to harass yourselves anymore to make it to eighty or ninety. Maybe just maybe you are able to relax and live comfortable on what you already possess.

A greedy person will never be satisfied, for things will never do the trick. We will never be happy by owning things and yet half the world is occupied with worrying about owning, so that tomorrow they can be comfortably fortified. It is an obsession and a hungering and thirsting for the things that never will satisfy. There is a fountain opened for the thirsty and unfulfilled which is Christ Jesus the Saviour who gives living water that wells up in a fountain of everlasting life and then the thirsting is satisfied for good.

Since we cannot predict precisely the future, it is not foolish to try to plan for it. It is better to hold lightly onto it therefore than to be straining tenaciously for it. Let go and let God do the planning for you. If you are not there yet then start learning to trust His word and hear what he says. He has promised to take care of the birds and the lilies how much more He will take care of His children. It is a misnomer to believe we can do the job and do it correctly. Of a certainty, I know that what I am suggesting is from experience. He is more than adequate for the caregiving and He does it with great pleasure. If it is His pleasure to give us the Kingdom, how much more then will He be pleased to supply our daily needs. God is our friend and our Father and He gives liberally, therefore if we acknowledge this fact why should we worry in the least. Be strong dear believer and know that His word is true and trustworthy; let us not doubt any of it.

CHAPTER 13

SELF-CONTROL, THE ESSENCE

86 A reinvention in many cases is necessary in our lives. We need to take stock and proceed with caution. Mapping out a realistic paradigm and follow it closely. Knowing what we need to be happy and go for it in a timely manner. Never be anxious but moving surefootedly and securely at our own pace until the attained goal is reached. Peace and happiness will be our companion. Many ideas and customs need to be left as unnecessary baggage. We need to travel lightly as the runner who prepares to run a race. They are unencumbered by any excesses. We need to clear our minds and thoughts of the things that clog it right now and move on with our lives. We need to indeed reinvent ourselves. We must, like the car manufacturers turn out a new product that works better than the present one. Each succeeding day therefore, we progress a little or become a better person judging ourselves by what we did wrong yesterday and endeavouring to change for the better each succeeding day. This is living purposefully and not carelessly.

A good life is not a piling up of goods as some seem to think. Differentiate yourself from the crowd. Leave the Joneses alone and move at your own pace. We all need our own pace and time to climb our mountains and we must not be dictated to by anyone.

You and only you are busy writing your chapters and especially the last one better be a good one or else all the previous ones written will be forgotten, for the life will be judged heavily by that last chapter. Of course, the one you are writing now better be considered the last one, so make it a memorable one. There is no greater pursuit than to find your true self; discover and develop that true potential the reward will be satisfying. I am saying this because this sounds or reads like my autobiography. I have endeavoured to do just as I am suggesting.

Let us be up and about, storing things which are of eternal value and not possessing that which retains only diminishing value. Todd Riley coming to his senses once said: *"What I spent I had; what I kept I lost; and what I gave I have."* This is a provocative statement or expression of his life. He came to realize that nothing stored down here can be of any lasting value. Heaven is where the seals will be used to legitimize our treasures. Whose seal do we want to stamp our treasure the Lord's, of course?

Certainly if we seek success in time and eternity then we must assume Godly objectives: Setting our affections on things above and not on things down here on earth. For those who think there is nothing beyond what they can see and hold will of course be losing all? Their treasure will be burnt up finally because they will not stand the test of the fiery trial. Under the scrutiny of the fire all their works will be dross and come to naught. As Christians we are building on a firm foundation: Jesus Christ the Rock of our salvation.

Courage is a great and mighty word and the secret of freedom emanates from courage. Courage will undoubtedly separates us from mediocrity and propel us into new spheres of living we have never known possible. We can enjoy freedom but first we must have the courage to separate ourselves from things that besets and shackles us. Even in the midst of difficulties one can shine forth as a beacon. The

87 Latin term: *"Ad Astra per Aspera"* to the stars through difficulties is the motto of courageous people. They are undaunted in their pursuit for their splendid dreams. These are the people who are confident that in spite of difficulties or setbacks, in the end, the difficulties will be surmounted, the problems solved and then declared: "Duty done." Not easy but the determined soul yoked together with our Saviour will overcome.

We have all been given a winning hand at birth and many of us gamble it way carelessly; we have all been given a turn at the helm of life and many have run a drift on the reef. We are existentialists; we are responsible for the outcome of what we have been given. There is no blame to be attributed to anyone nor will anyone take the blame. We alone are responsible to pull up ourselves and make good.

As a matter of fact, most of the answers you are searching for are hidden in your own mind already. I am not trying to teach you something new if you can read these words you are on the way to becoming an overcoming person. We are able to rise above every circumstances and difficulties; walking in light of Micah 6:8. *"He hath shown thee, O man, what is good; and what doth the Lord require of thee, but to do justly, and to love mercy, and to walk humbly with thy God?"* If we heed this exhortation, we all shall do well. We all will prosper and prevail and subdue every debilitating circumstance. Let me reiterate; we are not slaves but masters and overcomers. This is our status in this live and in the life to come; we shall reign and rule with our Lord.

Revelation 5:10 states: *"And hast made us unto our God kings and priests: and we shall reign on the earth."* Is this prospect a daunting one or is it a glorious opportunity to be somebody. Why should we wither and die at such a prospect after death. We should rejoice at the eminent entry into the door which is called death. D.L. Moody looked through that door before he left this life and said: *"It is glorious."* If we fail to actualize this glorious entry into our new world, we simply have no spiritual sight. Let us look at another portion of Scripture and read what is laid out in our future as believers. This is a blue print if you will of our future. Revelation 22:5. *"And there shall be no light there; and they need no candle, … and they shall reign for ever and ever"* let us not show one hint of hesitancy to trust Gods word and be afraid to leave this earth. Let us not waver between two opinions especially when some of us have lived our lives already; there is not much more that we can do to affect the outcome of things down here.

I might try to encourage you to do what you know to be right and true but you have already grasp the importance of what is wholesome and right but imagine what you will begin to envision and experience when you learn to imagine a new life. Now are we walking humbly and securely with our God and this is a marvelous new life. Let us embrace it, caress it tenaciously with all our being.

It is there for the taking and each of us has the ability and the intellect to effect the necessary changes in order to see better results. Life is like learning to swim. When one has mastered the art then less energy is expelled in crossing from one side of the pool to the other. We all learn effective strategies to accomplish the same task and when we become perfectionists we are way ahead of the game. We become masters of our journey travelling with the minimum of baggage and enjoying life to its fullest.

88 Each progressive day and year we can become better at what we do to add to the quality of our lives. So now we say up and up and away. We are on our way to a more meaningful life, we shall dwell in the atmosphere where the air is refreshing and the wind stays at our backs. If not why not? I say why not because we owe it to ourselves to carve out of life a comfortable place to dwell. Go for it. If we embrace *"truth"* truthfully; as a person who will stand fast for what is right and honest and moral and be willing to suffer for it, then we will have come a far way into managing ourselves. If we be that person, then we will not faint in the day of adversity because we will be living in light of the reality of life.

We will know that anything is possible in this sin cursed world and because it is not our home we will endure.

Be ye reconciled to God

A call to affirmative action: 2 Corinthians 5:20. *"…we pray you in Christ's stead, be ye reconciled to God."* In verse 18, Paul states that we have been reconciled to God through Christ Jesus. That is a statement of fact and in verse 20 he is stressing the need to be reconciled to God. The need to stress reconciliation I believe is that some might have wondered out of the way of truth. He also points out that we have not only been reconciled but we have been given the ministry of reconciliation. When Jesus in His ministry showed mercy He is teaching us also to do just that, show mercy also. We are His disciples when we begin to practice the things he did and practiced. We are now the salt, the preservative and the light pointing the way. How can we not be seen and felt.

How often we fail to see the depth of the language and the gravity of the sentence or phrase. We gloss over some most important passages of Scriptures and it does not inform as it should. The most important warning we can get is from the Bible but first we must believe in the One who sent the message. The message of the book called the Bible is to a lost world and the essential message is to find our way back to God. The word reconcile is that word which is to bring in line with; to balance the books in Accounting terms. The word reconcile in general is to make friendly again after an estrangement; harmonize, make compatible. It is giving us again our rectitude; our moral right standing with the Father Who Himself is righteous and cannot have fellowship with the sinner without this reconciliation. Paul pleads with us to actually do what we are commanded to do, for without it we remain alienated from God and the fellowship which we were made to enjoy in the beginning. Are you in that right position of reconciliation?

Many might think nothing of this warning and dismisses it as trivial in the scheme of things but far from it, our eternal well-being depends upon it. We must be reconciled to God and that is through His Son the Lord Jesus Christ. Unless we are brought in line with God there is no hope. This is the same word we learn in Accounting. Before any posting is done to the General Ledger the journal has to be reconciled. This is basically a balancing act if you will. Both the Debits and Credits must agree.

89 No one can begin to understand the strength or the magnitude of this word until you have personalized it. Until one is reconciled to His Maker, we walk in total darkness and lack that moral uprightness that we are possible of exhibiting. I make this appeal to you the reader because I have experienced this reconciliation and I shudder at the thought of not having being reconciled and its consequences. It is never a trivial matter. A take it or leave it attitude. It is a matter of life and death.

The sum total of our lives will either be eternal life or eternal separation from God with no appeal throughout all eternity. Without salvation, the most intelligent and industrious intellect would have lived in vain.

Whatever words I use or do not use, the truth remains the same, I urge you not to procrastinate untiltomorrow. Get on your knees now and ask God to forgive you of your sins and grant you His peace. Like the prodigal son going home to the welcoming arms of his father; my Father will do the same for you. He is waiting to welcome you home. Home is where the heart is at ease and everyone is family. Come!

1 John 1: 7 tells us: *"The blood of Jesus Christ His son cleanses us from all sin."* That is the purpose of His death to pay the penalty which is required for our sins. Now it is paid, we can again take our rightful places with our Father at the table. Every time a sinner repents there is a band striking up in Heaven. Yes! There is rejoicing in heaven every time a sinner comes to Christ. It is not so much that a converted sinner becomes such an asset to

God and His Kingdom. No! I rather believe that the reversal of status and location is a greater reason to rejoice. I rejoice myself when I have pointed someone to Christ and they have repented. I thank God for saving them from everlasting damnation; from the everlasting burning. The prospect of entering into Heaven as described in the Bible is reason to be jubilant but even without such a reward, I would rejoice just to escape Hell as it is described in the Word of God.

Hell is a place to be feared and to be shunned. Jesus Christ gave His life and everlasting life comes to us now as a gift. This is a gift like no other, that the God of the universe Himself could give His only begotten son to redeem mankind to Himself. It is something hard to fathom but the proof is there. He came, He lived and died and rose again for our justification. Justification puts us in the position of being just before God. When we are justified then it is as though we had never ever sinned. That is our new standing before God. Consider the hilarity of this matter dear Christian. God does not remember our sins. He cannot remember when we were sinners and He cannot look up our records either, for there is none. Now we have no record. A dear brother before his conversion of course, had committed a heinous crime for which he served time. After his conversion he wanted to go on the mission field and applied to the Queen for pardon. It was granted and he completed his studies and went to South America with his wife as missionaries. He told me personally as we worked as Beekeepers that he has a son-in law who is a Cop and he asked him to search the records for his conviction. After some time the son-in-law told him that there was none because he could not find it. It was destroyed. If our Father tells us that ours too are destroyed, why would we still search for it?

We must endeavour to aspire to new heights and cultivate a right attitude toward living that kind of life, the life without sin. Simply put a sinless life. If we do, we will be unmoveable and we can move with

90 confidence through life. We will be ready to shake off every disappointment and difficulties that come our way and not live in the shadow of yesterday but in the light of today with a glorious hope in tomorrow. To control any outside forces or anyone outside of ourselves is tyranny and we do not want ever to live as tyrants but as honorable forgiving and compassionate persons taking care of the person who we can best control and that is ourselves. If indeed we cannot take care of this one self, then it seems odd that we could take care of the least outside. We can be comforted by the foregoing as we tread this journey through life down here and no matter how dreary life becomes, we must dwell richly in hope; for if we do not believe the things stated so far, we are robbing ourselves of what is truly our inheritance. This is a rich and prosperous life, the new life in Christ; let us live it to its fullest.

Let us make that our objective and never lose sight of it, to improve the one who is worth improving that is *"Self."* Ask the question as you venture on this new life. Would the child you were, see anything to emulate in the person you have become today? Ask that question and if you have a satisfactory answer then keep up the good works and keep on improving. It shows that you are on the right road to happiness and success. I say success in that when one can control themselves they are mighty indeed and successful.

Proverbs 16: 32 declare: *"He that is slow to anger is better than the mighty; and he that ruleth his spirit than he that taketh a city."* We see the display of self-control and supremacy displayed everyday as we travel through life. Someone flying off the hammer as we say at every little incident, whereas another person would lose his finger his arm and not say much except to grunt. My friends, power is self under control. Why can't more of us be that person? We can I am sure, I am practicing what I preach here and I am getting there, God helping me.

We must accept responsibility for our future and until we do, it is all left to chance. We can build our own bridges to success by entertaining ourselves with learning and revising. Most of us have been bogged down by our own lack of desire to succeed. There is a tide in the affairs of men and we must find it and ride it. It is not always there for us but it will show itself one time or another. Many of us practice the greatest time saving device ever and that is procrastination. Tomorrow I will do it but *manana* never comes. Start now on something new and challenging no matter how small and once you get in the habit of learning you will be challenged to continue. A new language perhaps is a simple enough thing and then you go to another and another and before you know it you have built a desire and a routine for learning.

Emma Wheeler Wilcox left us a great inspirational poem to help us get over the doldrums when they assail us.

> One ship sails east
> The other sails west
> By the selfsame wind that blows
> 91 Tis not the wind nor the gale
> But the set of the sail
> That determines the way they go.

There is an equal opportunity for all of us and I am speaking to most who are not hampered by some social status where it is impossible to survive let alone to prosper. Putting those circumstances aside, we who live in the free world seems to have time in abundance and yet we squander it liberally. We indulge in hapless activities year after year and have nothing to show for it. We become settled in our ways and stay there. In essence that is not real life although it might feel good. We can improve our status and we can be something of consequence. You will go to the gym and see people there from one year to the next and sure enough you see the results. They have grown from a skinny fellow to a man whose physique you envy. Why is that, they have a heart to succeed at this particular thing. So can you and me.

Nothing is really hard; everything is simple, no matter how hard it looks. If it can be done then you and I can do it. Somethings may take longer than others but what if we come in last no shame on us. As long as we are in the race that is what counts. You and I are becoming better persons day by day as we know a new word in another language. Progress is the operative word here. As long as we do not remain stagnant and irrelevant but progressive and up to date we are progressing. We might be on the right tract but if we do not keep relevant we will get run over, we must keep moving.

Consider the new world which we have entered in since the fifties. Before then it seems that the world was practically at a standstill. With the exception of a few notable inventions, most things that we enjoy or utilize today are brand new; invented since then and there is now such a proliferation of inventions, we are panting to keep up. Most of us can barely turn on our new stove and so on, not to mention using the other more sophisticated gadgets. We cannot master all that is new but we strive to keep relevant nevertheless by some indulgences.

One day I watched two young men at the beach with a surfboard and the first man got onto itand immediately sank and the other took it from him and glided over the water effortlessly. Was it the first try by the second man I suppose not. He sank on his first try also perhaps a long time ago but he never gave up, he persevered until he could make the water work for him just what he wanted to do.

Knowledge is worthy of your attention and your most meticulous pursuit. It is what differentiates the pretenders from the real deal. It is the most sought after of all pursuits. Knowledge keeps a person strong and vibrant. It is not money and fine jewellery, those things do nothing for lifting a person, it is what's within that counts. Knowledge legitimizes the real person and puts him in the forefront. It is not your size nor your looks, it is knowledge. In today's world, knowledge is the most powerful possession

92 of all. It is a must for the ambitious person. Everyone wants it; power that is. Knowledge leads us to wisdom which gives us mastery over our circumstances. Seek after it and you will do well.

I am too old to learn you say. Well at twenty five I thought I was too old to learn but it is after that that I earned several Diplomas, Certificates and a Bachelor's Degree. I am in my seventies now and learning is the most wonderful pastime or recreation I can think of. It is most rejuvenating for me to say the least. Never stay static or you will fall back; keep revising and refreshing your memory and you will find pleasure in living. Life must be refreshing and enjoyable every morning you awaken, or you will have no reason to get out of bed. You only are responsibility to establish that pattern of refreshing your memory day after day, no one will assist you. The libraries and the bookstores are packed full of books for our learning and enlightenment so why remain ignorant about so many things?

CHAPTER 14

AS STUBBORN AS A MULE

We are all born with the proclivity to have our own way. We are stubborn, selfish and undisciplined; we all like to be left alone and unmolested, sharing our gains only with ourselves. The child always resist with a no and the mule do not want to be harnessed either. Those children running around and demanding everything are of little pleasure to their parents, their only language is: Give me, give me. The mule runs wild and makes havoc of things without harness and training also. They are all alike without discipline. However, when disciplined, they all become a force for good. The child turns out to be good fathers and mothers and the mule a wiling worker, always pulling its weight. Both the animal and the human with training show great potential and demonstrate power under control. Discipline is therefore the operative word here.

Without discipline the river becomes a swamp and a ditch becomes a grave. All of life needs channels and we need to guard those channels and secure the fences. Fences are there to keep out intruders and walls to buttress and keep in valuables. We need to guard ferociously what God has granted us as Christians and not to treat it lightly. The things we consider precious we know how to take care of them but some of us treat our Salvation as though it were of little value. We must remember the cost to our Saviour. The world at large sees the trivial things as worthwhile and the everlasting things as worthless. On the contrary, we as Christians see things in their proper perspective; we view things from an everlasting point of view.

In spite of this view of eternity, we treat lightly the gift that was given to us at such a price? Most times we live in a state of despair and wantonness to say the least. We ought always to rejoice and praise God for our new found faith and not to allow room for self-pity and murmurings. As Paul points 93 out, we ought to strive valiantly to keep the faith which has been entrusted to us. It is a precious possession that we have and we must guard it securely with all our might. God help us to see it as it is.

A meaningless array of thoughts and philosophies can lead us in a sea of despair without a vision and guidance from the Higher Power. We like to speak of a great spiritual force pervading all things without any real purpose and aim but to hear of the One who demands, prohibits and commands is another story. That thought we do not want to entertain because we are stubborn and undisciplined. We simply want to have our own way and not be held responsible for our actions. Some of us need to be reined in and put under the bit and the bridle to keep us on a straight path. Our God is not a tyrant, a hard taskmaster and will not subject us to a tyrannical rule, He gives us a lot of rope, a lot of leeway and we can live our lives as we see fit. He commands but He does not demand our allegiances; that has to be given freely and out of love. I will say it again. Jesus Christ has given His live for my sins; the least I can do is to live for Him. This is my conviction. I do not need a dangling carrot to follow Christ nor do I need to be coerced into doing so. The benefits already received by following Him are enormous. The fact that I am not in the world anymore, taken out at twenty two is enough to keep me singing.

It is not in the camp of the man who outrightly rejects God or denounces Him as none existent that the trouble lies but among the religious groups. In this group you hear that God is a merciful God and will not neglect any for their efforts in serving Him. They claim that although they may not come in the name of Jesus Christ yet they hoped to be saved. They are counting on His Mercy or hoping for a change of His heart at the end. God has already stated that His word will not change: Heaven and earth will pass away but his Word abideth still. We cannot presume upon God and assume that He will be favourable to us when we have neglected to do what He says. Repent is the call word, repent and be save so that your sins will be blotted out. If that has not taken place in your life do not hope for anything but to hear the words "Depart, I never knew you."

In John 5:24, Jesus said: "*Verily, verily, I say unto you, He that heareth my word, and believeth on Him that sent me, hath everlasting life, and shall not come into condemnation, but is passed from death unto life.*" If you hear the words of Jesus Christ and it causes you to turn to the Father then you have eternal life. That is a done deal but if you shun His words and think little or nothing of it you are left out in the dark. The Bible declares all throughout its pages that without the shedding of blood there is no remission of sins. Christ shed His blood that whosoever believeth on Him may have eternal life. That is the Gospel. If you have not accepted this provision made for the washing away of your sins, then your sins remain. No sin shall enter heaven. The person entering must of necessity have his or her sins washed away by the blood of Jesus Christ. Find out how if you do not yet grasp the import of this message.

If in the end, God goes against His word by admitting everyone, saved and unsaved how trustworthy would He be? Not very would I say. Consider studying hard for an exam and in the end, everyone passes, the kid who never takes up a book gets his certificate just as you who sits up many nights cramming all you can absorb in order to pass. How fair would that be to you who had studied very hard?

94 That would be tantamount to a rotten system. None would be happy with such a system. This is an analogy, analogous to God allowing everyone to enter heaven. He simply would not be just and we know that He is just. His justice sent His son to die on the cross to pay for our sins which we could in no way pay for ourselves and which if kept, ultimately demands death and separation from God forever.

Freedom, the buzz word

Freedom is the operative word of our day. Everyone wants to be free from the shackles of responsibilities and live without real purpose, not submitting to any authority. Civil disobedience is everywhere; it has become a buzz word. Citizens are quick to rise up for one cause or another, even if that cause is just saving a battered cat having only one life remaining. The other eight have been spent. Humanity wants to express its anger against everything and everyone. The status quo is not working because they cannot get what they think they deserve from it. Everyone has his or her entitlement and that is freedom to demand whatever they desire. We have seen the havoc which they have caused upon the world and the strain that they impose upon governments those that are strong enough to subdue and deal with the rampage of this marauding bunch. They are everywhere on the planet. They are on a rampage and are bent to destroy and in many places they have succeeded in toppling governments. Sometimes some good have emanated from their actions but mostly it is a set back and more suffering is piled upon the existing suffering. These are the people who think of no higher power and believe that they are able to institute the changes they desire by themselves. God is still in charge and He will be until that day when He steps in fully to institute His government. We want to live free now and not worry about responsibility not to man let alone to God Almighty. The deceptive thing is that we think that we are succeeding in having our own way. Far from it, we will answer for every deed done in the body while we abide here on earth. Those of us who are repentant sinners will know that our responsibility is to our God and His word and that while we labour here we must be obedient to our laws and governments. We give unto Caesar the things that are Caesar and unto God the things that are God's. The path we take is not ambiguous; it is clear, God helping us to find it.

Establishing deep roots

The earlier we find our roots and establish them in good sound teachings the better off we will be. We will have established those roots never to be uprooted because they are established in "Truth" and not error. There is a manual available which is a guide for our well-being and longevity and it is the Bible. Many scoff at it but it is the best investment you can make in time and expense. It has worked for me for over fifty years now and its treasures astound me day by day. A God faring life is worth all the riches

95 in the world, it gives serenity, confidence and protection. We are kept abreast of current event as it pertains to the end; the approaching of the second coming of Christ. With such an awareness we live as the people we are: Pilgrims and sojourners in a land that is not our permanent dwelling place. It is in this light or realism that we live as Christians. We have a handle on the correct interpretation of what is taking place right now. Our eyes are opened and ears attuned to every movement of the world. We are in the now and have inside information as to its progress. We have been directed into the way, we should walk uprightly as obedient followers.

Jesus the one who created all things recommends it: In Mathew 6:33 He said: "*But seek ye first the kingdom of God, and His righteousness and all these things shall be added unto you.*" God's people were seeking after the things of this world and being anxious about their welfare and future and Christ criticized them that those things were the concerns of the ungodly and not for those of the household of faith. We have a heavenly Father who sees already what we have need of and is concerned about our welfare, so we must not be anxious about our future. Many of us Christians have found ourselves right there in the mix and in the thick of things as far as worrying and providing for our future is concerned. I can easily verify the fact that God is able to take care of us. I have been proving it for the last fifty years and I am not a bit anxious about my future. As a matter fact, I look forward with great delight each day for the blessings that are coming my way. They are enormous and I wonder at times if I am favoured by God and yet I know that that is not so. He has no favourites; He treats each of us equally and loves us with the same everlasting love.

There is great joy emanating from the actualization of God's love for me. In addition there is bright hope for the future for I know the one who holds my hand is the one who also holds the future. Just as the child and the mule have that proclivity to go their own way, so we too have that natural bent to be rebellious. We are hard pressed to acknowledge the fact that we are connected to God. We were created in His own image and therefore we are literally His offspring. Paul warns us to let the mind of Christ be in us. Nevertheless the world is rift with little gods. Pantheism says c.s. Lewis: *"Is the condition into which the human automatically fall when left to himself."* We fail after a time to see and acknowledge the transcendence of God. We are ever crying out, we do not want to be managed. We can manage by ourselves and managing ourselves is a lie. There is enough evidence to show how we have played havoc when we take over the reins and try on our own.

We think that it is all about us and do not grasp the gravity that God is a self-sustaining God and He does not need us. He existed before us and will exist independently of us if he chooses to. What we have as children is an added benefit to get closer to

Him in love and fellowship that is a privilege we now enjoy as children. I heard a Pastor declared that when he was ordained to the ministry he did not take the title Reverend. He felt it presumptuous since that was God's title and not man's. Yet, so many delight in such a title among us. Jesus Christ warns us about those who delight in being called Rabbi, Rabbi. When we begin to see ourselves as we truly are; insignificant feeble creatures then we will begin to magnify and glorify the Lord, whom we will see as Isaiah saw Him: *"High and lifted up."*

96 I have heard it said that we are like filthy rags before God, referring to the Christians but that is not so. Before coming to Christ our righteousnesses are likened to filthy rags and not ourselves. We are now clean because of the Word and as such we are vessels of honour fit for His use. 2 Timothy 2:21 declares: "If a man, therefore, purge himself from these, he shall be a vessel unto honour, sanctified and meet for the master's use, and prepared unto every good work." Here it is, a horse now of a different colour. No longer, "a slum dog" but a useful vessel prepared unto good works. That is now a marvelous transformation which shall make us shout for joy, being made clean enough to serve.

Many are serving and think by serving they will gain status or favour with God but far from it, He will not use us until we first bow in repentance to Him. It is only after we have been made clean, that we are of any earthly good to the Lord God Almighty in His kingdom. God can hold our hands and lead us into an everlasting and a glorious life if we would but acknowledge and submit to Him. It is His desire and pleasure to give us the kingdom. The restoration of fellowship is what the Gospel is all about. It is not as we say 'Rocket science' The smallest child can understand it.

I do not necessarily believe that we were created to serve and worship God as a potentate but as part of a family; a father and son relationship. After all, we were created in His own image, or in the likeness of God: that is, we possess the quality of personhood.

The essential characteristic of God is relational. He desires to have fellowship with his creation and that is us. The angels he made to worship and to serve and minister to Him in a different capacity from us. He includes us as a part of the family and that is what we are a part of: "The family of God." Let us delight in this new family, every day of our lives and play our part as honourable family members.

A natural tendency to be lauded

Men liked to be honoured and placed upon a pedestal but God forbids it. Christ who is God, speaking of men who liked to be called Rabbi, Rabbi, forbids it and says: *"And call no man your father upon the earth: for one is your Father, which is in heaven."* Mathew 23:9. My God and my father; is this true or not, that I can use these two words in one sentence and are they really interchangeable? I am sure it is true. My father must be as He said, a jealous God. Not wanting us to call any other man, apart from our biological father, father. Well!" How about that" borrowing a friend's phrase. Not everyone can call me father. This title is restricted to my kids only. This is the structure of our societies and the family of God is no different. The Christian can and do say God my father. How can anyone miss this great and marvelous and whatever adjective one can conjure up to express our elevated position in God through Christ Jesus. How can we miss it? How can we ever be down in the dumps when we can say; God our Father?

97 That is not all that we hear of our father which is in heaven. Paul said in Romans 1:7. *"To all that be in Rome, beloved of God, called to be saints: Grace to you and peace from God our Father and the Lord Jesus Christ."* This is a greeting Paul used frequently to salute the saints or brethren. See them in 1 Corinthians 1:3 and 11 Corinthians 1:2.

When I just got saved and spoke to a man of a different religion he criticised me severely for calling myself a son of God. Of course many speak from their own feelings and not from the word of God. As a Biblicist I am now well established in the Word and cannot be fooled or subjugated for I know the message of the Bible. I spend time in it daily. This is a truth, that in it are the treasures of wisdom and knowledge. We read in Colossians 2: 2-4 *"…and unto all riches of the full assurance of understanding, to the acknowledgement to the mystery of God, and of the Father and of Christ; In* whom *are hid all the treasures of wisdom and knowledge. And this I say, lest any man should beguile you with enticing words."* We have much of that today, enticing words; words that betray the truth and promote their own interest but you who are reading this book right now be prudent as in all other things and search the scriptures for yourself to see if the things you receive are what is taught in the Bible. We are diligent in other things, why not the most important message to the human race.

It is humbling to me that the one who is high and mighty can come to live in me. Isaiah 57:15 states; 'For thus sayeth the high and lofty One that inhabiteth eternity, whose name is Holy; I dwell in the high and holy place, with him also who is of a contrite and humble spirit, to revive the spirit of the humble, and to revive the heart of the contrite ones." That the high and lofty One can indwell me; astoundsme as much as it delights me to say the least but I know it is true for the experience is real and not an illusion. He walks with me and comforts me in my distresses, no longer is He a far off but now more than ever, I feel His presence.

CHAPTER 15

MAINTAINING A HOLY LIFE

Maintenance is the key to the usefulness and longevity of any product, machinery or our person. My first job with a mining company had different departments and one was a distinct department called the P&S (planning and scheduling department). It was the function of that department to schedule each piece of equipment for periodic maintenance. It could be a tune-up, an oil change or a transmission check. These were heavy equipment used in the mining of the bauxite and they were expensive. No expense was spared in the maintenance of these machines especially because of the cost. It is therefore assumed that the more the worth of a piece of equipment the higher the cost of maintenance.

98 We all as car owners know also of the cost of maintaining our vehicles. We do periodic check-ups and oil changes etc. and the costlier the vehicle the more one fusses about it. When I owned a little VW bug I never changed the oil I only added to it but as my cars became more expensive I followed the manual and did the maintenance according to the book.

This entire preamble is to come to a more important point and it is to show us that as Christians we have the most precious and costly of anything in the entire world and that is our souls.

Our souls are eternal and indestructible; nevertheless we need to protect it from harm. We can cause damage to our souls which will have dire consequence when we live and indulge in activities that we are forbidden to indulge in. As children of God, born again Christians we are warned and even forbidden to indulge in the things of this world. The things of this world, meaning simply, worldly things distinct from spiritual things. Many will mock and say it is not good to be too righteous but the command is given to us and it serves us well to adhere to the warnings. It is best to steer clear of many of the indulgences of this world though they are benign. There are enough things on the safe side for us to enjoy that we do not have to cross the road or the track or the bridge.

11 CORINTHIANS 6:17 states: "Wherefore come out from among them, and be ye separate, saith the Lord, and touch not the unclean thing; and I will receive you." When we bow to the command of the Lord we will do well, our souls will prosper and find rest in the Lord. The falling away begins when we indulge in the very things we came out from in the first place. If indeed we are now a peculiar people and a holy nation if we go back to sampling the worldly things it is said we are like the dogs that go again to their vomit. If we value our most precious possession then we must guard it with all we have. We must maintain and keep it in mint condition. Let us start now to develop that habit. As I used the analogy of the car, and if our souls were cars, it would be the Rolls Royce of them all.

Maintaining a Holy life means that we must live holy in the presence of a Holy God. We live in His presence by maintaining a meaningful prayer life, a Bible study so that we might know what is there and that we can defend our faith. In other words, we must know what we believe. Our faith is based upon truth and trust in a Holy God. It is expressed clearly that God favours those who trust in Him. If your faith is a vacillating one, God will not favour you when you come to Him in prayer. I have come to this conclusion because of what He says in Psalm 37: 40. *"And the*

Lord shall help them, and deliver them: he shall deliver them from the wicked and save them, because they trust in Him." A condition for receiving our answer to prayer is because we trust in our Father. This is not an outlandish expectation but a reasonable one. We can get what we ask for because of our connection with Him.

99 *Projection and Forecasting*

Projection and forecasting is not the purview of Corporation and Industries and other Businesses alone but it is for the individual as well. Albeit in a small measure we all ought to project and set goals. If we do not, then we find ourselves falling behind the times and even drifting listlessly through life. We need goals and a definite purpose to carry us on from day to day. Getting through a day with little or no activity is a killer for me. I must be engaged in some meaningful activity or I would suffocate and die. Engagement is the life blood that stimulates us and keeps us sane and I know, I speak for many when I make this statement.

Sometime ago I heard a man calling into a radio station telling the host that he had learned a new word for the year and to him that was a real achievement. Learning a new word was big to a man but how many others do not add anything at all to their vocabularies but loses some of that which they knew little by little as the years go by. It is so, that if we do not use it we will lose it. Little wonder that so many are suffering from dementia; too little activity they engage in to sharpen the mind and to keep it oiled. Many have not come around fully to the realization that the whole body needs taken care of; not only the physical but the mental as well, among other things of course. Setting goals and forecasting is a way of maintaining and adding to our growth and our worth. Some years ago I read a statement put out by the VW motor company that in a few years they would become the number one car maker and I followed that prediction. Today as I write this statement they have achieved that status. They have taken over the number one spot from Toyota. This they have achieved in spite of a scandal which rocked them for several years costing them Billions of Dollars. It was a rigging of a pollution system in their Diesel engines.

In spite of the road you are on today I want to encourage you to take stock and get on the high road. John Oxenham has set out two ways for us and I encourage you to take the highway.

> There is a way and a way and a way
> The low soul takes the low way
> And the high soul takes the high way
> And in-between on the misty flats
> 100 The others drift to and fro

But to every man there opens a highway and a low And each decides the way his soul shall go.

In the West where we have grown up with the Christian religion we simply take our heritage for granted in that we easily gloss over things of eternal import. The idea that we as Christians can relate to God as our father is foreign and almost sacrilegious to other religions of the world. In a book *"I Dared to Call Him Father"* a wealthy Pakistani woman, Bilquis Sheikh whose religion was not Christian would not dare to think of God as someone who would be interested in having fellowship with mankind. Of course this is how the story started. God and our first father Adam talked together as man to man in the Garden of Eden. That relationship is restored again in Christ Jesus.

Bilquis Sheikh was introduced to our God and when she submitted to Him and found out that it is true that she could enter into a relationship with Him, she was shocked. When the relationship was restored and realized she declared: *"Suddenly a breakthrough of hope flooded me."* Like many others before and after her, this experience and realization are being experienced daily by those who would believe. It is true dear readers, when

I have a problem which is beyond me I plead with my Father to take care of it for me. It is true that God the Creator of the universe wants to have fellowship with us and invites us to do so. There are many who doubt that that is so and even doubt the existence of God Himself. There is a reality which evades a lot of us including members of the household of God and that reality is that we do not place ourselves inside the circle where we belong. We are all part of that round table if you may, fellowshipping and planning as it were with the head of the household our Father. He is strategizing with us, bringing us up to date with future events but do we want to listen? Such is our position in God; we are privy to his workings but we must present ourselves at meetings and listen for directions.

The French Philosopher, Mathematician and Physicist Blaise Pascal states that: "People most invariably arrive at their beliefs not on the basis of proof but on the basis of what they find attractive. He argues that a rational person should live as though God exists and seek to believe in God." He further advances an argument come to be known as "Pascal's Wager." It posits that all humans bet with their lives either that God exists or He does not. The wager in its most succinct form is as follows: "If one bets that God does exist, and He does, you win *"everything"* to lose, you lose nothing. Should one bet that God does not exist and wins, you win nothing,

101 but to lose? You lose *"everything."* Therefore, the man who believes that there is no God has nothing to gain neither in this life nor the one to come. He loses all around.

Some people would have the evidence staring them in the face but still will not believe. They are what we call die hard. They will not believe though one came back from the dead to declare the truth. A vivid example is that the co - discoverer of the DNA (deoxyribonucleic acid) Francis Crick denies in his autobiography, *"the design argument."* He would not acknowledge that for anything to be so complex there would have to be a designer.

Science writer Nancy Pearcey and scientist Charles Thaxton have had extended discussion of the significance of the discovery of DNA. One result is that it has given fresh evidence for the *"Design argument"* They have discovered that the amount of information discovered in a single human cell, equals the entire thirty volumes of the *Encyclopedia Britannica* several times over.

Many are willfully ignorant and refuse to submit because they do not want to acknowledge the truth that there is a Supreme Being. They would rather believe the lie that they are that being.

Now this is staggering for the mind to grasp. Many years ago when technology was in its infancy stages and ideas were only dreams and a bit farfetched it was envisioned that the entire Bible could be written on a single chip, one square inch. We could hardly believe it. But it came to pass. In light of these staggering inventions man place himself at the top of the universe and think himself as supreme master not even as co-creator. In so doing he has dammed his soul and destined himself to eternal torment.

In 1986 I went to "Expo 86" in Vancouver and one of the exhibits was information technology. One company showed off its genius by filling in the valley between two mountains in a matter of minutes with information to fill that space with books and yet man who is so very smart would still not believe that there is a power that transcends everything. It is the hubris in us which blocks such recognition. We fail in spite of the overwhelming declaration by the cosmos itself that there is a Supreme Being. To our detriment we fail to give God His due but that failure does not diminish His worth by the smallest atom. He still stands majestic in all the world. Our God is simply an Awesome God.

No matter what walk of life you are from or what status you now enjoy, to believe in God is the highest joy you can attain. In our day, eminent scientists from several fields are writing in support of belief in God and shunning the Darwinian theory of naturalistic evolution. What I seek to do in this book is to draw your attention to the reality of things. All things are not vague

10 as some see them. There is a time when reality grips us and grips us hard. The day when we are so distressed that there is no available help and there is no one but God to cry out to. You will need Him then but it could be too late. This is why I am here pleading with you to get to know Him now as your Father and friend. Grow a relationship with Him while it is possible and you will not regret it.

That the majority of the population should fail to see and acknowledge God as creator is to them a great loss, an eternal loss, a grievous loss, a damnable loss but for those of us who believe and fail to see that we are: *"A chosen generation, a royal priesthood, an holy nation, a peculiar people; that ye should show forth the praises of Him who hath called you out of darkness into His marvelous light:"* 1 Peter 2:9. It is to our loss also that we do not reach our full potential in the relationship. Whereas we should grow in the grace and knowledge of our Lord and Saviour Jesus Christ we remain stunted and undernourished. There is water said the Ethiopian Eunuch to Philip, *"What doth hinder me from being baptised?"* There is light says the Bible: What is then keeping us back from being illuminated and even full of light ourselves? What manner of persons ought the Christian to be? Should we be easily distinguishable from the rest of the world by our behaviours and our indulgences? If not, why not? Should our speech be different; courageous and kind, hopeful and salubrious or should it be clouded by pessimism and fraught with criticism? We must work out who we are; a people who are peculiar and of royal priesthood are easily detectable. There should be no doubt about it.

I was driving a TTC bus one day when at the stop there was some pushing and one lady who tried to move before another was accosted and rebuked. Her reply was: "You are lucky that I am not of this world or else I would give you a box." She is saying that she was restrained by her Christianity and yet she should not find herself in such a situation in the first place. She should not be fighting for the first place but giving up her place instead.

We are the great losers when we walk instead of riding. Kings ride and not walk. Footmen walk and kings ride. As a Christian, do you merely exist or are you living triumphantly above all the circumstances and difficulties that confront you. Do you learn to lean heavily on the Lord who is the source of our strength? I am throwing out these questions to challenge you to live up to your heritage as I am endeavouring to do myself. I know it is possible and I have been experiencing His closeness for many, many years now and I am constrained to challenge my brothers and sisters to do likewise.

In Revelation 2, there is a message to the Church at Ephesus that God knows its labour, its works and its patience but there is a warning amidst this seemingly healthy congregation. 2:4 *"Nevertheless I have somewhat against thee, because thou hast left thy first love."*

103 Is there a standard set for the Christians or not. I do believe there is a standard set for us and we would do well to find it and follow it. In this portion of Scripture we read that we are neither hot nor cold and as such we will be spewed out. God wants us to get back to basics; He wants us to get back to the time when we just got saved. Everything was new again and we have not maintained that stand or kept that attitude instead we waned and faltered over the years and that is sad.

We have to get back to the source and be recharged for the journey ahead or else we will depart as defeated and disheartened soldiers. We need to enter triumphantly and we will do so only as we maintain a holy life.

Will we be saved as by the skin of our teeth rather than making a triumphant entry into His Kingdom. An abundant life is the purview of the Christian, nothing less than that should satisfy us. A triumphant life is our right, it is our heritage and our strength; if we fail to see it, we are short-sighted and if we see it and fail to follow through, then, there is another problem which I cannot diagnose. May God help you to see the problem that hinders your progress?

CHAPTER 16

REJOICING IN HEAVEN

Rejoicing is a great theme running throughout the Bible. In essence an emphasis is put on that word because of the infinite worth of our souls. We on earth rejoice when a great battle is won, a great or valuable possession has been found or restored, a child is born and the list is endless. We are emotional beings and as such we are elated when something glorious happens to us or our love ones. It is equally true when we suffer loss or defeat; we are saddened and despair sets in. These are two extremes in life, rejoicing and mourning.

Someone has said there is always good news but the bad news is that the good news is slow in coming. We live with the bad news as a norm but the good news are scares and far between, nevertheless that is really what we live for "Good News." The birth of a baby, passing an exam and winning a trophy etc., these are the things that keep us sane and buoyant.

Satan's business is still big business, growing and thriving and behind every evil, every activity that rages against the Word and God's servants is the Devil himself. He is super intelligent and

104 is the ruler "*...of the darkness of this world...*" *and of* "*...principalities and powers...*" Ephesians 6:12. His business is to seek whom he may devour. We might admit that He is good at

devouring because He is making mincemeat of so many even some supposedly seasoned veterans. Satan's devices as cunning and subtle and are not blatant as some might think. He is like the cops. They do not hang out a sign telling us where they will be when they conduct a blitz. Their intent is not to warn you but to catch you in a wrong.

Back to the topic of rejoicing however; against this backdrop we can see the reasons why there is great rejoicing when a sinner repents and turns to God.

In Luke 15 we read of the lost sheep, the lost coin and the lost son. The lost son is a theme which we can all enter into as parents. We invariably have had such a situation be it a son or a daughter. As such, upon the return of this child we would not spare anything to lavish upon that child, naturally we would go all out to welcome that child back home and to let them feel at ease again. A party with friends is the thing to do to bring about the satisfaction from the overflowing love of a father or mother.

That there is rejoicing in heaven over a sinner that repents; we can only speculate as to why there is such rejoicing in heaven when a sinner turns to Christ. Is it a wondrous thing or marvellous thing when a sinner repents? Is not God's power greater than Satan's and yet there is such rejoicing nevertheless. There is a good reason for rejoicing. A soul has been snatched from the hands of the enemy is cause enough for the rejoicing. Forever Satan has been denied this soul and that in itself is a good enough reason. But consider a rescue in the middle of the day when one has been surrounded by the enemy. Now that is worth rejoicing over. God has dramatically snatched you out of the enemy's hand and that is worth a celebration both here and in heaven. You might be able to add to the reasons why there are celebrations.

Picture yourself living beside an alligator infested river and having children. You are always busy with your household chores as a mother of four or five and having a toddler who has no awareness of danger. One day as you came down the steps of the house you see an alligator crawling up the bank of the river and you were just in time to snatch your baby who was outside on the ground playing or simply crawling around. How would you feel for the rest of the day and for the rest of your life? This is an analogy to show the reasons for rejoicing in heaven. A soul has been delivered from the mouth of the destroyer hence the rejoicing.

A soul is a priceless possession for it is a person's eternal possession. It is indestructible and last for ever and for ever. A father or a mother might rejoice at the death of their wayward and reprobate child. They might be relieved at the end of their onslaughts on society, of their

105 debauchery and shameful lifestyle but contrary to man, God does not delight in the death of the sinner. The Bible tells us that God has no pleasure in the sinner's death.

Ezekiel 33:11 tells us: *"Say unto them, As I live, saith the Lord God, I have no pleasure in the death of the wicked; but that the wicked turn from his way and live..."* Throughout the scriptures the warning is given and the invitation is to turn and live. That is the Gospel. It is a message of Mercy and Grace. *"For God so love the world that He gave His only begotten son that whosoever believeth on Him should not perish but have everlasting life."* John 3:16. If turning to Christ was purely an act of God then everyone would be saved considering that He does not delight in the sinner's death. I have come to realize that much is riding upon us and we can decide the way we want to go. God through the death of His son has made it possible for everyone to be saved. But there is still resistance to his offer. Not everyone is willing to take Him up on His offer and He is not about to force anyone to accept it either, that is the way I see it anyhow. He so loved but He does not force us, He only invites us and whosoever will may, *"come."* I believe that that is love when God lays out two roads before us and distinctly labels both and giving us their destinations and the value of both destinations. So then we decide the way our soul shall go.

We are fully informed about both places; on one hand the comforts and blessedness and on the other, the degradation and ruin. Who then will be able to point a finger and say that God is not just, for He has not given us choices? No one will be able to. As I speak to people about their souls salvation, I will hear them pointing finger and asking what about all the other religions, are they going to Hell too. The glorious or good news of the Gospel is that it does not discriminate. Every religion, every race and every tongue are welcomed into the family of God upon acceptance of the Lord Jesus Christ. Upon repentance and acceptance of the work done upon Calvary's cross, one is saved. Jews and Gentiles, bond and free alike; no exception.

It is not made difficult for anyone, all are welcome and the door is set as the place of entry into the Kingdom. Jesus is the door and if any man must enter he has to come through Jesus Christ. On the contrary, those who refuse to come that way have forfeited any chance of entering the Kingdom. Access can only be obtained through the front door; it has no backdoor or side door whatsoever. Noah's ark was a place of safety also and it did not have but one door, the front door and when it was shut it was shut; all entry was then denied.

Yet some would say they will not trust a God who will send a person to Hell. Well with all the warning and invitations if one makes it there they do so on their own volition. The rich man in Hell cried out, asking that someone be sent to tell his brothers so that they might not come there. The Lord says, though one came from the dead, they would not believe. Christ came back 106 from the dead and they are still not trusting Him. Felix said; come back to me some other time and I will listen. It is not stated that Paul went back another time and he believed. It is never a convenient time for many, for they are too busy grasping after things they will never use or dissecting a truth that they will not punctuate.

I once witnessed to my own mother and she told me that she was born for hell. Well glory to God, wouldn't you know it; she repented long before her death. I remember going there at the old home and she would say to me: *"My son, aren't you going to read the Bible to me."* I never ceased to pray for her and thank God He answered my prayers. As I am on the subject, I might as well tell you about my father as well. He too accepted the Lord as his Saviour in his old age. I know I will see both of them again in Heaven perhaps sooner than I thought.

Too many are too busy today sending down roots here on earth and are oblivious that their lives are but a vapour. They say: "I have worked hard for six days and Sunday is all I have for myself and my family.' God who gives the strength gets no time not even an hour. Everything else is too attractive and alluring. The ball games and the cottage and the whatever: Every cent is spent on self and family. The poor can remain in their misery and die because they will not spare a dime to supply even a cup of clean water. Every cent is squandered on themselves and their families. That is the extent of their world, their families and circle of friends.

The thing that is lending procrastination to the mix is called distraction. There are a thousand and one things invented as distractions by the Devil to keep us away from the main issues of life. Imbedded in the Scriptures are the treasures which will lead to eternal life but we must be willing to dig for it. As the miner digs for diamond and the sculptor hammers on an unyielding rock day after day before he sees any real likeness of what he intends to make, so must the child of God labours in the things of God daily. It is a laborious task but it bears sweet fruits and the reward is out of this world. Christian, let us be up and doing as commanded; time is short.

God is not willing that any should perish but that all should come to repentance. God desires that all be saved but because He has not made us as robots programmed to do as directed He has given us a choice. He has placed two roads before us, the broad and the narrow and He has told us where both leads and we make the choice as to which we will take. God has given us all, intellect and we have the ability to recognize right from wrong. I believe that God has demonstrated His fairness here that He did not bound us over to Himself because He has paid through His son's death on the Cross the penalty for our sins. He did not say now you are all mine for I have bought you back by the sacrifice of my son on the Cross. Since in Adam all have sinned then in Christ all should be made alive again but it is not so. It is whosoever will. Although the Lord is showing Himself and calling men and women by name as He did Saul of 107 Tarsus, please do not wait for a special call. Most of us did not get that call. It was through the preaching of the Word that we bowed the knee.

I could have said: "Some other time I will bow but not today, or I could have decided that I do not want to follow Him; I want to continue in my ways, it suits me just fine." I would simply be making a decision to reject Christ and remain in my sins. Many cried out on that faithful day: *"Crucify Him let His blood be on our shoulders."*

It is not an unfortunate thing to reject Christ, it is not a regrettable thing; it is a damnable sin; a sin for which one is condemned in Hell forever. One might ask, why should a finite crime be punishable by an infinite punishment? Because it is rebellion against God and this is infinitely immense and immeasurable. It has the same weight as the angels who rebelled in heaven and were cast out and that is a permanent loss which they have suffered as it will be for anyone who rejects Christ now.

Having choices can get us into all kinds of trouble, we indulge and interpret things that ought not to be interpreted but should only be accepted. When the Bible speaks of a place of torment then we reasoned that the dead cannot be tormented. If one is dead then one knows nothing anymore and so on. If there is everlasting torment then one is made alive again to feel and suffer that torment. There will be the resurrection of the dead both great and small, saved and unsaved. We need to take time to meditate on these things, digest, and ruminate on them as a cow would on the grass it eats. These are weighty matters worthy of our full attention.

Today's society is busy inventing their standard of living, and allaying God's standard little by little. There is the old adage: *"If you tell a lie and repeat it long enough it will sound like the truth."* Take this one: *"Money is the root of all evil."* There is a thought that is rampant in our society which is named "Situation Ethics." Situation ethics is a thought based upon circumstances and not upon any absolute moral standard. Such principles will get a wrong doer off any charge backed up by a good lawyer. In other words, everybody is getting away with murder these days. There is one murder one will not get away with and that is the murder of Jesus Christ. It was your sins and mine that nailed Him to the cross. Remember?

We have been inundated with such arguments, that there are no absolutes that thought is very pervasive in our society today. Many have swallowed those lies but the tests comes back to haunt us in the long run. When we have tested the ideas and eventually come back to embrace the absolutes, sometimes it is far too late for us to make sense of it. We get away from the notion and reality that there is a God and embrace a self-centered lifestyle which is the heart of humanism. There is a school which was started by John Dewey an atheist who was the first president of the school known as *"American Humanist Association."*

108 The American Humanist Manifesto reads, *"As nontheists, we begin with humans not God, nature not deity. No deity will save us; we must save ourselves."* Many people want to hear such statements so that they are let off the hook, so they think. How very convenient. To say there is no God absolves one from any responsibility toward a *"Supreme Being."* One can easily live without God in their thoughts, although it is not a worthwhile thing to do. It is like living without a lot of necessary things in our lives. We can live without life insurance but I would not recommend it. We can live without fire insurance but again it

is not a good idea. The day fire hits or you suffer a severe health problem is not the day you can get either of those commodities. If you suffer any of those losses without coverage you are left out in the cold.

I would compare living without the acknowledgement of God as driving a car without brakes. Yes, you can drive a car at any speed without brakes but if and when you have to stop, then there will be severe consequences. Coming to the end of ones rope without God is a fearful thing. If when you are alone in your little corner and that will happen as sure as night follows day and there is no comfort for your journey into the next world it were better for you never to have been born. Many have lived bravely but at the last lap or the last chapter fear sets in. No longer can they face the night without some light. It is dismal to say the least and many do confess at that point that they have put it off far too long and can no longer ask for forgiveness. They know now that they have crossed the Rubicon; all hope of turning is lost. On the other hand, the Christian facing the same circumstances know that in quietness and confidence is our strength. For we have trusted in Him.

These are proud men and women who in the face of such unquestionable facts while they prospered deny the existence of God. Let them be left alone but do not follow them into a lost eternity. I plead with you, think for yourself and fall on your knees and if your inclination was to resist God, please confess your sins right now. Ask Him to forgive you and set you free from such tyrannical and antagonistic attitudes. He will pardon you and restore you to sanity. You will be forgiven and clothed in your right mind once again. Pray Habakkuk's prayer: *"O Lord I have heard thy speech, and was afraid: O Lord, revive thy work in the midst of the years, in the midst of the years make known; in wrath remember mercy."* Habakkuk 3:2.

My God have mercy upon us. Even a man of God who worshipped and reverenced God at times is humbled by the awe of His grandeur. Consider Habakkuk's prayer, it humbles us when we realize the depth of his humility as he sees God as He is, majestic and great. Yet it is only the hem of his garment that is even visible; His entire being cannot be fathomed. God is worthy of all our praises and adoration, let us never cease to praise Him.

109 The men and women who deny the Deity of God will live lives of debauchery and dissonance and like the drunkard they will try to hide their troubles. They are not happy and can never be, for deep down in all of us is something which will not give us rest until it is purged. You guess what that thing is? It will not let you go and no man has a solution for that problem. The answer is not to be found in indulgences and rituals but in humble submission to the Almighty God. The Christian Gospel speaks of: *"Having our hearts sprinkled to cleanse us from a guilty conscience."* Hebrews 10:22. That sprinkling is through the perfect sacrifice of Jesus Christ's Precious blood. Anyone can have that application anytime, anywhere at no cost.

"...His blood cleanses us from all sin." 1 John 1:7. This is the only antidote for the sin question, the Blood of Jesus Christ. As in the past, stretching back to Adam, the blood of animals was used as sacrifice to atone for the sins, now the Blood of Christ is given up once and for all to satisfy that demand. No longer is a sacrifice necessary to atone for our sins. It was done on Calvary's cross once and for all. Those who have experienced the cleansing are truly free for the first time in their lives. No longer will they have to invent happiness but they are liberated from the shackles which bound them to this world and all its allurements. He, whom the Lord sets free, is free indeed. It is so.

Ask the Christian how much of this world's goods he needs to be happy and he will tell you "Little." That is the truth; his or her happiness does not reside in the things of temporal value but in eternal value. We were originally made to be free, as free as a bird but sin has entrapped us and enslaved us and we search again to find our own way of escape. There is no way out except through the Cross of Calvary. This fact has reverberated right down the centuries, men and women falling prostrate in confession before their Maker after a life of debauchery and rebellion. No one can hope to escape the burden without confession and repentance. The one, who rejects this provision, is forever lost.

Many cry out that they do not understand the Bible but how much time do they spend in it. How diligently do they search for the treasures hidden in it? Men invest time in the things they are most interested in and the things they think will give them the most satisfaction. They invest their life's earnings in a scheme which they believe will make them rich overnight. Rightly said your treasure is where your heart is. There is one place where we can invest where the winnings keep piling up and that is in the Lord. Invest in Him and there will be no loss.

J.C. Ryle observed and said this: "Be very sure of this, people never reject the Bible because they cannot understand it. They understand it too well; they understand that it condemns their own behavior; they understand that it witnesses against their own sins, and summons them to judgement. They try to believe it is false and useless, because they don't like to believe it is 110 true." This is a true summation of the situation by J.C. Ryle. Many would rather ignore the truth with the idea that it will not affect them in any way. They would rather think of it as only a dream that they will wake up out of. I would advise some of them to pinch themselves sometimes and realize that this life is real and it will come to an end someday. To so many it will be quite abrupt and they will not have the time to say Lord have mercy. It does not bother me they say now but behold the day comes when it means everything to you; the day when you will stand before the awesome God who will demand an answer. *"What have you done with my Son?"*

We have become so adept at problem solving that we now believe as a matter of fact that we are able to solve all of life's problems no matter how difficult. The great geniuses are slipping away from the earthly scene one after the other and I often wonder why. Why are they dying? Aren't we on top of our game? Of course, not; it is all an illusion. We are able to solve many visible and tangible problems but there are unseen things which we cannot even perceive until they are revealed to us. Without God's revelation, we are still so blind we stumble even at noonday.

There is the problem of the soul and that has to do with sin. Sin robs us of growth and happiness and until that sin is purged, our lives remain stagnant, half lived and unfulfilled. We do not or cannot reach our full potential until the burden and guilt is taken away. It is not until this sin problem is rolled away like Paul Bunyan's bundle was rolled away, can we envision and realize good spiritual health. We will not be able to surmount the problems we face; we must deal with them through repentance. That problem of sin can only be dealt with by the Lord Himself. Ask for cleansing and you will receive it and made new. That is the Lord's vision for us sinners. He is willing to make us anew and the price or provision is already in place. So what are you waiting for? Be renewed today.

I must reiterate that it is: *"Not by works of righteousness which we have done, but according to his mercy he saved us."* Titus 3:5. It is straightforward but if we do not know we do not know. Many are struggling under the impression that it is by works that we will attain to righteousness. God will favour us and give us a place in heaven by the good deeds we do whilehere on earth. If that were the case then it would be laid out clear in the Bible for us but that is not the case. If we will not see what is required and labour under the illusion that it is works then we will know the truth but far too late. It will not be until the judgement day that that fact will ring clear and true to us all but then for the unbeliever the time is past for help. It will be too late because eternity will have already been fixed and the destinations established. 111 Today I urge you; let the rejoicing begins, let the band be brought forth and the chorus ring forth… has come home, let heaven celebrate.

CHAPTER 17

WHY WILL YOU PERISH?

Why will you perish O man, because you chose to? It is so, because you chose to die. In life, you have embarked upon many projects such as becoming an Architect, a Farmer a traveller, a truck Driver and so on and you have had the courage to reach your destination but this, your most important venture you have no appetite for. Why not? You will not exert the energy to pursue and to wrestle and settle the most important matter of your existence. It is your soul's salvation or its welfare that is. You are encouraged now to give it your earnest consideration and attention.

I once witnesse to a co-worker who told me that that is what he pays his Priest to do; that is to pray for his soul. Just how many life threating situations would you entrust to your loved ones let alone your soul. There isn't a verse anywhere in the Scriptures which shows us or directs us to allow anyone to pray for our souls. In the Old Testament there were those appointed to make the sacrifices for atonement for men's sins yearly but all those sacrifices since Adam were only shadows of the one Great Sacrifice and that is Jesus Christ. Since His sacrifice, we have access to the Father. The access we now have is on behalf of our own souls. We may pray and intercede on someone else's behalf for anything including his soul's salvation but he or she has to go to God and repent for an effective salvation. It has to be personalized. Do not be fooled that someone else can absolve you from your sins. It is only God Himself who can and it is when anyone comes to Him confessing with their own lips that they are sinners and acknowledging to God that He is able to forgive that sin. Romans 10:9: *"If thou shall confess with thy mouth the Lord Jesus, and shalt believe in thine heart, that God hath raised Him from the dead, thou shalt be saved."* Please take time to read this portion in your own Bible and digest the message. It is your mouth, confessing your sins, to your God that will bear results. No one else can do it for you.

It is fallacy when someone thinks he can pray for another person's salvation. No one can do it. Someone else can pray and ask God to touch the heart of such a person so that he or she makes the decision or takes the step to follow Christ and that is all. Christ has to meet you personally and *vice versa*. There is no way around such an encounter. We need to know these truths before it is too late. We do not want to find out that we were being duped and deceived. Too many of us like to take the easy or the low road but it will lead to disappointment and a great loss. This loss of a soul cannot be recouped once eternity rolls. Your treasure will forever be lost to the devil that is busy deceiving you. Bear in mind that there are many deceivers coming in the name of Christ but they are none of His.

112 Jesus spoke of these people who are ravenous wolves and who are not only keeping themselves out of the Kingdom but are barring others from entering. Little wonder the word of God or the Bible is all about showing us the way that leads to life everlasting. God has no pleasure in the death of a sinner and the reason is that, that soul is lost to the Devil in torment for ever and forever.

You might ask, if God is sovereign then how is it that Satan could claim a soul. Throughout the history of mankind God has not dealt with us as robots. He has given us a will and provided us with guidance as to how we should relate to Him. Abraham is called a friend of God because he obeyed God. He was blessed because he sought guidance from God as he should. He had not rejected the guidance which God gave him nor neglected fellowship with Him. Man in general seeks his own way and as such wanders off into the dead of night and takes a way which leads to destruction.

Our father Adam disobeyed God and it resulted in sin. Since then every one of us bears the curse. If you believe this statement then you can read on if not there is no need to read any further. After the fall we are all in hell and now needed to be rescued. God devised a plan by sending His son to die for our redemption.

When the Christians engage the unsaved about their eternal welfare it is often shunned as a light matter. It is the weightiest matter in the whole world; Heaven and Hell that is. At death is the parting of the ways forever and forever. Our state is forever fixed then. Remorse will set in but there will be no repentance. If you read this I plead with you to believe it, for why will you perish?

There is the fork in the road, one leading to Hell and the other to Heaven. You will ask; has anyone ever come from Heaven to speak to us. Yes read on. Genesis 11:5. *And the Lord came down to see the city and the tower, which the children of men builded.* Heaven is the Lord's throne and it is up and Hell is Satan's dwelling place and it is down. This is the way they are described. Luke 16:23. Speaking of the rich man: *And in Hell he lifted up his eyes, being in torments…* Hell is a definite place, a location and an adress if you will. People live there, people are tormented there and people want to get out from there but they cannot. They cannot get out because they have missed the opportunity to be saved here on earth and this is the final place of their existence. There is a finality to all things, after this life and any opportunity to do good or bad will be lost after death. This present life is only an opportunity to make a decision about our eternity. Those who cease that opportunity are wise.

There is one who spoke to us from Hell. In Luke 16: 23 we read: "And in hell he lifted up his eyes, being in torments ..." This was a rich man the Bible spoke about who fared well here on earth ate sumptuously, wore purple robes and paid no attention to his eternal wellbeing and as such died and went to Hell. He had made his wealth his god and trusted in that wealth to do everything for him. If he ever considered living for God it was at a later date but now today is all one has. Tomorrow may never come. Many will find themselves in Hell because they have put off trusting Christ just a little too long.

Others of course, do not want to bow the knee to our God. They despise Him and as such choose Hell as an alternative so that in essence Hell is a place of their own choosing and Heaven is a place that they

113 would not want to go because that would be acknowledging God's sovereignty. Nonetheless, we must feel pity for them especially those we have witnessed to and others who are our mothers and fathers, brothers, sisters, children and grandchildren. I pray that the breath you have now dear reader you will use it to ask for mercy and have a sure future and a good destination. Heaven awaits your petition.

Live as an Existentialist

There are things we must consider and among the things which I have been trying to say, I have also endeavoured to produce proof from the Bible to substantiate them. These are not things that I make up from my own intellect

for mine is small. There are written that you and I might know. Many things are not mysteries. They are written plainly for our understanding and as I ponder certain passages I have come to the conclusion that certain terms logically follows that we are responsible for our destiny. The way we take is not predetermined by the Creator. The Lord knows where we are going in the sense that He knows the end from the beginning and as such he sees each of us as though we were already there.

He is the Architect and knows where each beam and post goes already in the building. He sees the finish drawing and knows what the finish building looks like. God knows who will bow the knee but He does not do it for us by forcing us. The Bible says that as many as receive Him to them He gave the power to become sons of God. There are no limitation; as many or whosoever. That offer seems quite liberal and expansive to me. How many times I would have been happy to come to Christ if once was not enough but it is. If indeed Christ wept over Jerusalem that they would not listen to Him, then it follows that we have a will of our own. We can refuse to believe or we can turn. If God does not desire that any should perish and since He is sovereign, then we could not perish. If we would be saved without our own involvement then Christ would not have to suffer as He did on Calvary's cross at the hands of wicked men. He would simply select whom He will and the matter would be closed. He has died for the *"whosoever"* may come to Him and humble themselves and follow. Each of us must see ourselves as sinners and embrace His love. His love and mercy is offered to all who hears the word but must receive it personally.

No one can receive the forgiveness and deliver it to you. There is definitely no middle man where salvation is concerned. We have to get our gift from the Hand of God ourselves. I believe that that is wonderful because in so doing we know we are getting the real deal, there can be no counterfeit in the process of receiving what is offered because we will take it directly from the Giver.

In all of life, we depend largely upon our fortitude to get us through life. If we join the military we work and endure hardships to the maximum to be able to be good enough for survival, in school we strive to be the best, in university we cannot falter either or we will be run over or left behind. Why is it then that when it comes to eternity we cannot make the effort or take the time to confirm this truth? Is 114 there life after death? Is this true and is it a pressing matter that each of us should grasp and embrace now.

Making a reservation for our eternity is a pressing matter and each sane person should set it as a priority because there are two things looming upon us: Death and the Judgement. If we all knew when any of these two things will be, then we can linger and make things right with our Maker just before we close our eyes in death or just a day or so before He returns to earth but other than that specific knowledge we would do well to do it now. Your philosophy has not reached its zenith until it comes to rest in God's truth or in the truth of God. Having a purpose for living is what makes the difference in a person's life. Is it a fruitful life or is it withering away day by day. We see it daily, the soul enlarges and strengthens and although the body decreases as it will, nevertheless, we surmount all the debilitating circumstances because of the hope that is within us. Living with "Hope" makes a fruitful life.

The confusion in the Camp

There is one whose job it is to discomfit and produce a dissimulation of information in order to lead us down the wrong path. There are too many denominations under the Christian flag that are gone the way of Caine. They want to project their own ideas over God's commands rather than accepting His word. Most are socially motivated rather than Biblically directed. They want to build a "Just Society" The Great Society" where equality is the norm. It is in essence building a social society where everyone is equal in men's sight and God is sidelined altogether. They are to be found in the dozens, all vying for a place in the spotlight of the world. They have found that the way of the Cross is too restrictive and as such, they are opening it wider to accommodate more people if not everybody. Great road builders are they. The Way of the Cross is narrow and restrictive where only a few enters and that is the Biblical perspective or teachings. It is demanding and has "Truth" as its tenets; God's truth and not man's wishes.

Man has become more humane than God in these last days and whereas God's edict says the sinner shall die, man's says the sinner shall not die. It seems rather contradictory that some in the Christian camp would even embrace the doctrine of no God. How can that be, we say. It goes to show that some are not willing to pay the price demanded, yet they are hoping to reap the benefits that Christianity offers. We must know again that what God demands is what we are going to pay. If He demands total submission to Him then that is what we will have to do and nothing else. When He asked for a blood sacrifice from Cain and Able and only Able responded accordingly, then Cain's was not accepted because he ignored what God had commanded and brought a fruit sacrifice instead. The pulpits are full of these men today bringing what they think is right instead of what God demands.

In 1 Corinthians 3:13 Paul points out: *"Which things also we speak, not in the words which man's wisdom teacheth but which the Holy Ghost teacheth…"* The Gospel of salvation is not about man's wisdom but about God's word and truth. *"There is a way which seemeth right unto a man, but the end 115 thereof are the ways of death."* Proverbs 14:12. How often man thinks that everything is about him. Of necessity God will accept him in the end no matter what he does. That is the pride in him which makes him believe he is quite indispensable but far from it, it is God whom all things revolve around. If and when we lose sight of this fact, then we are heading down a slippery slope.

Do we want to risk listening to man over God, then pay you will? In Matthew 25:41 we read: *"Then shall he say also unto them on the left hand, Depart from me, ye cursed, into everlasting fire, prepared for the Devil and his angels."* The road to Heaven is not being widened but the way to Hell is being enlarged to accommodate the large crowd rushing in.

If we are engaged in the fray then we should be involved with our sight set on the prize. We should be in the arena to win and not to lose. Many are giving only lip service to the Gospel of Christ and have denied its power. They shall not fare well in the swelling of Jordon.

I have come across many who say they believe in God but cannot accept the fact that Jesus was born of a virgin. They can accept the fact that God has created the universe but to believe that He was incarnated in the flesh is too farfetched for them. Could one ponder the fact that Christ could have come sitting as a baby on someone's door step and is brought up and cared for by that couple and then started His ministry? No one would doubt that. Of course His origin would be our preponderance. We would forever be wondering about His veracity. His birth was prophesied for hundreds of years and many were expecting His arrival and yet when the time came many doubted. A man would prefer to make his own god, one of convenience every time, rather than bowing down to the true God. How could one ever doubt that when such a one goes to Hell it is out of choice? It is going there deliberately; they go in with his eyes wide open, having been shown two paths.

It grieves the heart of God that anyone should not believe the truth but we are not robots programmed to perform a certain way. He has given us a mind of our own to reason and decide our own fate. If you have heard the word of God which calls you to repentance to follow and worship Him in spirit and in truth, then you are accountable to the Lord and responsible for yourself. If you have heard the Gospel of Salvation and turn away, then you have no excuse or any plea on that great day.

Joshua challenged the skeptics, the doubters and the hard of hearing, always vacillating; *"Now therefore fear the Lord and serve Him in sincerity and in truth...choose this day whom ye will serve... but as for me and my house, we will serve the Lord."* Joshua 24:14-15. Where are the truthful prophets of God today, proclaiming from the pulpits the whole council of God? Most are pacifying the dead instead of raising them from their state.

If you have been naming the name of the Lord Jesus Christ and not living in accordance with His commandments then it is time you start doing what is right. It is only a service of sincerity and truth that counts. The waywardness and deception in our lives will not advance the Kingdom nor help us either. Proverbs 4:23 tells us: *"Keep thy heart with all diligence; for out of it are the issues of life."* This is a warning to the redeemed to keep the heart pure. Keeping the heart pure is to keep it free from all 116 the impurities of this life. There are too many to mention but you know what sins you harbour in your heart. Purge those sins at the foot of the cross and ask for forgiveness and turn away from them and live as you ought to. You will be a happier and a more effective Christian from now on. Keep on the path of righteousness dear brethren. Strive for the mark of the high calling of God.

Those who believe in a certain world view that there are alternate truths are dead wrong. There are natural laws governing our universe and ignoring any will not help in the least. There are some under certain conditions who believed that they could fly and jumped from buildings only to realize that their beliefs simply defy the laws of gravity and as such met their deaths. North is always north and south is always south and so on. There are varying degrees in relationship to these points of the compass but one is either getting closer or further away from the true north or south. True North will always be true north so will Truth be. Let us keep in mind that nothing can be fully understood except in relation to God's creation and His divine plan for us and the universe; It is His universe not ours. He has a plan and we would better know it and live happily within it.

The Christians refuge and strength will always be The Lord God Himself and no other. There can be no variation from this principle. We must learn to trust Him and to do so implicitly. Our lives must become one with His. Now are we in Christ which means our lives are being controlled by Christ's principle. We are now Christ centered. *"Christocentric"* if you will. Who we now are surpasses what we do, what we own or possess, they all are but passing fancies. They shall all pass away like a mist under the sun's rays. Our hope of survival is in the Lord and it is only what is stored in heaven will last. We must always to be vigilant and fervent in serving the Lord. It is simply our reasonable service to do so all because He created us and bought us back for Himself through the Blood of His son.

Attempting to serve God without first submitting to Christ as Saviour is useless and futile. In fact, all the good we think we are doing in His name, in this condition are described as filthy rags. That is the reason the Bible denounces such things as worthless, in comparison to the Gift of God which is eternal life. We do not cling to those values, earthly values that is, to the exclusion of the eternal. We must hold the value of things in their proper perspectives and in proportion to their values. The Gospel offers a more glorious life than the one we now have. It offers faith hope and love. If we are in Christ we are now dwelling in love for God is love. Faith in Christ indeed moves us altogether into a new sphere of life and living. It reunites us with our Father whom we were alienated from and that alienation was not because of our sins committed yesterday or since birth but went back to Adam whose sins we inherited.

We must come clean as it were, repent and serve God as the redeemed of the Lord. There is no other way in which we can have the peace which was promised.

Our lives now as Christians are no private affairs but have become a public spectacle for the world to see. We do not live one life different from what the Bible teaches. We do not have a private confession and a public vocation. Whatever we now do we do as unto God. There must be no secrecy in our lives but so live as though all were exposed for criticism. Let it all be exposed to the scrutiny of the public and as such we will seek to build a more generous, peaceable and loving existence. Let the public eye be our 117 critic. Of course whether we are conscious of it or not they are our critics. They are critiquing our Christianity every minute of our existence and rightly so for they need our light to see themselves.

Oh the impudence of the unbelievers who prefer their own gods and come to solicit the help of the Almighty in times of difficulty. The impudence is palpable to say the least. Those outside of Christ who are tragically prideful and will not submit should not merit our scorn or ridicule but our pity. Some are more afraid of physical suffering than of the corruption of their eternal souls. *"Rejoice, He who is great in power is your friend."* Spurgeon. How wonderful to know that that is so. God is the friend of the believer, the person who trusts in Him. We can confidently call upon Him in our distresses. Having read this you undecided reader, why would you perish?

CHAPTER 18

LIVING THE PRETENCES

The falsity that exists among us today is of mammoth proportions. Those who embrace spurious religions are many. If you cornered one such person they will be offended at your inference that they are propagating a wrong faith. They would consider you rude and inconsiderate to want to guide them in the right way. Then I have heard from the pulpit that such division and criticism is harmful to the Gospel as though we should all unite and settle in and preach. The spurious mixed with the errors andeverything will be fine. I personally believe that falsity must be denounced and be separated from.

Men have the inkling to cling heavily to things they hold dear to traditionally. It takes much wrenching sometimes to separate them from old customs and ideas. The truth will be glaring, nevertheless they hold fast to the old ways. Nothing short of a miracle will turn their minds so that they might see their error and embrace the truth. Even to point out the error we are criticized for being critical or judgemental. "We must not judge, leave judgement to God," quite so, Judgement is God's purview but we must be discerning and shun the errors and correct them when we can. If we fail to act and to correct where we see error and deception we would be hypocrites. We and popularity are worth nothing in light of the Truth. Christ and His word alone must be promoted and elevated to its fullest dimension, only then can we be satisfied that duty is done.

May God help us to be brave enough to point out errors, so that when anyone makes it into Hell, we did not assist them?

We live a lie constantly and play parts that we are not. We live as millionaires when indeed we are ordinary wage earners; proletarians and not bourgeoisies. We identity with many things false and we feel good about ourselves living in those roles. Each person is bearing three identities: One is being the person other people see us as; the second, the one you pretend to be and the third, the person you 118 really are. The one you go home to sleep with at nights and wake up to face each morning that is theperson you are. That is the person that is worth your full attention and many times he is the one who is most lacking he gets the least attention. We must be careful to portray the correct self at all times.

I once spoke to a friend about his religion and the deadness about their doctrine and he acknowledged that he knew but he continues in it anyway. It is in our nature to live under pretences. Some of our marriages no longer work, our strength no longer exists, our wealth is diminished and we pretend as though everything is all right. We carry on keeping up certain appearances and that is all. Then in the end who are we fooling, no one but ourselves because who cares how little or how much we pretend to have, nobody. Before God, we are not what others think we are, not what we would like to be but who we truly are. We may remain opaque before men but to God, well, we are all crystal clear.

Martin Luther a devout Catholic could not find peace in his soul in spite of all the penances and devotion to his church and his superiors. When a person cannot find peace they search and search until the light breaks through. There is enough light out there to illuminate the whole world. There is a cloud of witnesses attesting to His magnificence and greatness. How can we miss it? Mahatma Ghandi once said: "All around me is darkness and I am praying for the Light." He knew of the Light of the world but he did not submit to the Light, otherwise he would testify of the Light. That is the experiences of many, they know of Christ but they will not personalize the experience. They will not commit to His authority.

A Gallop poll cited in *"Church Around the World"* of December 1989 claimed: "Eighty four percent of the population firmly believe in Jesus Christ [while] ninety four percent believe in God." This must be a North American statistics. Then those who believe in Jesus Christ are of two categories; the ones who believe that He was an historical figure only and the other who knows that He is God incarnate. He was born, He lived and died. That is as far as some will go. The second set knows that He is God and worships Him as such. The pivotal matter, the crux of the whole matter rest here; *"Who do you say that Christ is?"* He is the enigmatic figure of all ages; to some, He is the Christ the promised messiah and to others a stumbling block, they cannot get past Him. How can we not know when it is all laid out in the Bible? The promise of His coming, His coming, His departure and His eminent return are all laid out in black and white. Look at the array of information and some are still looking for His first coming.

For the sake of clarity, let us examine who the Word of God says He is; where He stood before He walked among us and where He is today. Let us look at the records and decide for ourselves. Here we open the Scriptures or the Bible to John 1: 1-4. "In the beginning was the Word, [Jesus Christ] and the Word was with God, and the Word was God. John 2: The same [Word] was in the beginning with God. John 3: All things were made by him; and without him was not anything made that was made. John 4: In him was life, and the life was the light of men." These are only some of the things set forth about Him, not to mention the numerous prophesies which foretold of His coming into the world in the flesh.

In John 1: 12 we read: *"But as many as received him, to them gave he power to become the sons of God, even to them that believe on his name."* Some find this hard to understand that humans can be sons and daughters of God but it is set forth here in black and white that we are sons and daughters

119 when we believe in Jesus Christ as God and not as a mere man. That we are now in the kingdom and live in His presence as a family with other believers, calling God our father and Christ our friend is a magnificent truth indeed. That is the *Status Quo* but things will not remain in this state. The same Christ who went into heaven will come again at a time appointed by the Father and then there will be the culmination of all things. That time is near and we would do well to prepare to meet our God. Amos 4:12 declares: "… *prepare to meet thy God."* This is an ominous warning to the unbeliever, the ungodly if you will and no one else. He has been given a reminder, the warning to heed God's word and turn to Him or face the consequence which is everlasting banishment from His presence.

The prophets wrote of the Lord, the people witnessed Him personally, two thousand years ago and the next time we shall encounter Him is when He comes again as the conquering Lion of Judah. John tells us this in Revelation as he saw it in a vision: *"And I beheld, and heard the voice of many angels round about the throne and the beasts and the elders: and the number of them was ten thousand times ten thousand, and thousands of thousands; saying with a loud voice Worthy is the Lamb that was slain to receive power and riches and wisdom, and strength and* honour, *and glory and blessing."* Revelation 5: 11-12.How awesome is that scene my Christian friends? We simply cannot wrap our minds around such an event.

In light of the foregoing, the Christian cannot therefore indulge into sinful practices without the realization that each indulgence has a pernicious effect. We ought then to purify ourselves and be holy as He is holy. Christ has given himself for us in death, the least we can do is to live for Him. This is my testimony. "I will live for Him as long as my breath remains." Dear reader, the lord Jesus Christ who died on the cross for our sins is worthy to receive all the honour and glory that we can afford Him. He is truly worthy to receive that honour. Why should anyone burn when there is such a cloud of witnesses and warnings, attesting to His presence, why would not we return to the Father where victory is truth, dignity is holiness, peace is happiness and life is the hope of eternal life with God the father for ever and ever.

Martin Luther found no peace in his soul in spite of his devotions to his church. Finally he declared: "When by the spirit of God, I understood the words, *"The just shall live by faith"* I [was] born again like a new man; I entered through the open doors into the very paradise of God." His search had ended then for he had found the very thing he sought and that was peace with God. It is the Scriptures and its words that liberates. Our peace is not in tradition or religion but in God's truth. 1 John 1:9 says: *"If we confess our sins, he [Jesus Christ] is faithful and just to forgive us our sins, and to cleanse us from all unrighteousness."* No one can even begin to imagine the joy and assurance that comes to one's heart and life when at last that which they searched for is granted. Peace with God. Not only do we have God's peace, which passes all understanding but we get added value as well; we now have power with man and with God. This is a wonderful fact.

Like Martin Luther, we will all get what we ask for if we ask in faith believing. Instead of our sinfulness and unrighteousness, we are now given a badge of honour which we can wear freely without 120 anyone peering over our shoulders. Now for the first time we have been set free from sin and its guilt, no one can from now on accuse us of sin because we do not have a record. In the books of heaven where it matters, we have no record. Whom the Lord set free, is free indeed. Freedom is knowing experientially that there is nothing between us and our Saviour. We have been reconciled to our Maker and the books are balanced so is the scale of justice.

He got what he was searching for all his life and when he got it he would not give it up in exchange for his very life. The rest of his life after getting his prize was to share it with others and to try and expose the delusion that so many were under that man could exonerate us from our sins. If man could absolve us from our sins, then Christ's death would not have been necessary. Think about it. Everyman himself needs to repent and have his sins forgiven and there is only one who can forgive our sins; Jesus Christ.

Having received something as valuable and as priceless as eternal life, Peter warns us to: *"Sanctify the Lord God in our hearts."* 1 Peter 3:15. Why this warning by Peter because he knows the magnitude of this matter, that what we have is to be guarded and protected with all the ability and ingenuity that is within us. He wants us to set the Lord apart in our hearts as the most important matter and person there is. We should dwell on Him in every aspect of our lives. Show Him as the one central magnet of our being and aspirations. Let Him envelop our very being, as the water envelops a swimmer when he gets in it.

In temporal matters such as sports, one sees the tennis players devoting themselves wholly to the practice of tennis, the golfer to golf and the boxer in training. These people will seek out any avenue and uncover anything that will give them an edge over the opponent. They literally live and breathe their crafts. In the arena of life, the Christian or Saint has an opponent most cunning to deal with and the better equipped we are to deal with him the sooner we can reign supremely over him. We must reign in life and show the world that we are victors and not victims. We must bring every besetting sin under the blood of Jesus Christ. Let Him deal with all our shortcomings and frailties, for He has commanded us to bring them to Him.

I have heard the story of a sports star whose team won the super bowl and immediately after the game he went on the telephone and ordered a lambergeni and fell back on the couch and confess his emptiness. He was just show but no substance, he seemed as the macho man and yet inside he was lonely, empty and afraid. Like many others, he was living a lie; he was putting on a show an impressive show which he and God know to be a lie. Again we need to invoke Matthew 6:33. *"Seek first the Kingdom of God and His righteousness and all these things will be added."* Until we have God first and foremost in our lives, all other things will not make up for the loneliness and emptiness. We were made to have fellowship with God. That is what reality is, pure and simple.

Men such as Freud who asserted himself as the persuasive cunning of a powerfully gifted literary man, said that all faith, all belief, is an illusion bred of childhood fears. If ever it were possible to interview this man in his abode now, I would love to ask him a few questions. First I would like to ask him if this statement is his. Perhaps his answer would be that he cannot remember making such a

121 statement because he would be too embarrassed to own it. He who considered himself to be wise turned out to be such a fool, being now in torment. My second question would be: "Sir! Are you happy with the outcome of your life? I would not need that answer for his condition would give away his answer. Where are they now? While they lived they belittled the source of power and influenced millions who also sided with them, acknowledging their spin on things as truth and have become neighbours in a hot place. I once witnessed to a co-worker and he quoted Freud and said: "You must have read him too." As if he was some god. Freud like so many other so-called brilliant minds have fallen by the wayside, kicked about like a little brazil nut. So they think they are smart and they have not the spunk to look up and observe the signs of the times.

Never mind the eloquence, if they come in any other name but the name of the Lord Jesus Christ, let them be anathema. Claiming to be wise but fools they are; now languishing in torment. Please dear reader do not practice in the same arena as those pretenders, live a rich and full life, trusting in the words of Jesus Christ. *"Seek ye first the Kingdom of God."*

CHAPTER 19

CHRISTIANITY ORIENTS US FROM THE COSMOS TO THE UTTERMOST

If conditions were as they should be in this world which God has created then there would be no need for interventions. We would dwell happily and every person would be well pleased to do the pleasing things to their God. Things are far from being ideal and the reason is that we are under the influence of Satan the god of this world. It is his DNA that the world bears. There has been a change at Calvary, however, a cataclysmic shift if you will from one DNA to another. Now the child of God who looked to the Cross and believed that Christ the promised messiah took his sins on that cruel cross shall now bear God's DNA.

Without acceptance or connection to the Cross of Calvary we are all floundering. If however, we make the connection, then we are no longer vacillating between two opinions, no longer are we dimorphic, the cross and its meaning is no longer vague but is now crystal clear to us who have humbled ourselves and submit as the thief on the cross did. *"Lord remember me:"* Now are we the sons of God who believe. Today in your present state today in my present state we are sons and daughters of God. There needs not be any further qualification. We are now adopted and brought into the family of God. It is explicitly stated in 1 John 3:2. *"Beloved, now are we the sons of God, and it doth not yet appear what we shall be: but we know that, when he shall appear, we shall be like him; for we shall see him as he is."*

122 I am now the son of God and this is all I can bear. The news is too great for me. It is astonishing to know this immutable fact. I rejoice at the measure of love which the father has bestowed upon me and as such I strive for the prize of the high calling of God in Christ Jesus as I walk the pilgrim pathway, I find it a more glorious path to tread day by day. The light which guides me shines brighter each day thus making the pathway brighter and lighter. The struggles which beset me last year are now something of the past; it is so because I am striving to follow my Saviour in spirit and in truth. Each day I move a little closer to my Father. This closeness emanates from the wisdom I gain each day as I delved into His letters to me. How else would I gain that confidence that He loves me except that I read His love letters?

As I ruminate upon this wondrous love which my Father extends to me, I conclude why not, was it a light thing that He died for my sins to redeem me from the hands of the enemy. It was not and I must walk worthy of such a sacrifice for me. It is out of pure love that He came to save us. God help us all to understand the gravity of such love. This realization right now is like a ray of sunshine and I am basking in it, never relinquishing the thought that it is permanent.

Along with this revelation that God loves me as His son comes also the realization that the fall made it impossible for us not to sin and now the redemptive life makes it possible for us not to sin. God be praised. Mankind again have mastery and dominion over sin; no longer is he a slave to sin and this is astonishing news to the world at large and especially to those in whom the Spirit of Christ is vested. Hence the Christians are oriented from the cosmos to the uttermost. This is the best news this world has ever received.

*"For God so loved…"*John 3:16.

The statement: "For God so loved the world that He gave His only begotten Son that whosoever believeth in Him [Jesus] should not perish but have everlasting life" is so elementary that it has almost become too simple a statement to have any weight. A worn out phrase to many today. The historicity of Christ's birth and life in this world has worn thin to many and others are so obstinate in their hate toward the Lord Jesus Christ even at the mention of His name that the darkness, the blackness veiling their faces is palpable. The invectiveness that exudes from their very presence not to mention their language condemns them to the very recesses of Hell. How can they escape? They will never if they remain in their present state. It is in this light that the message of the Cross is a simple one that many are scrambling to find new interpretation for the Scriptures. Many are inventing new programs and adapting new strategies to attract sinners to Christ. The, "for God so loved…" is not sufficient they think.

Are erudite men and women who refuse to acknowledge the truth of God's word as relevant and consequential, happier than the poorest of Saints? Consider the joy that emanates from the presences of a Christian even with the meagre means to live by. Not hurried, not harried not anxious, and always moving confidently along because our happiness comes not from this world but because of an investment into the next. We are moving toward our treasure and not regretfully leaving it behind.

123 In a class at York University I encountered a professor who denied the Jews' journey from Egypt to Palestine or the Promised Land. He commented that the Bible account of all these people and cattle travelling for forty years and not a single person has even seen one of them. How very deceitful you must be to cast such disdain on the written Word of God. There will be special places for such people in eternity apart from the ordinary Hell

that we read about. Will any such persons have any objection for their rejection? "Depart" I think not.

God portrays Himself as a merciful God; He sends showers of blessings that we can see and enjoy, these are things that the grateful heart knows. He gives us a will of our own to choose or to reject anything and everything. It is up to us. In His dealings with men He has shown that He will break our stubbornness and bring us to our knees when he chooses to; such as the case with Saul of Tarsus. He sent Nebuchadnezzar king of Babylon into the fields to live like an animal for seven years until he came to realize who was supreme. He does whatever He pleases but the general invitation is out there and the word is our guide, we must know it and find its truths. His special dealings with men are His prerogative. He does what he wants and we all cannot expect every favour while we remain in our sins. He sends the word to you in as many forms as you are getting it and it is up to you to respond to that message. It is by that word that you will be judged; it is God's word, believe it.

Many men are distressingly stubborn, recalcitrant in their beliefs and it will only be after they are languishing in Hell that it will dawn on them that Christianity was the true philosophy and Christ the ultimate Philosopher. We do not fight for dominance or supremacy but rather we strive to bring men and women into the kingdom by entreaty and benevolence. Such is our approach, we make an offering and one is free to take it or reject it. We pray that one would see eternity as a definite place where they will be when this life ends and our desire is that they will not go to the place of torment but to that of enjoyment instead. Knowing the terror of God, we persuade men everywhere to repent. This is our objective, this is our burden.

The truth for those who finds it, is liberating, it is rejuvenating and refreshing; it moves one from darkness to light, from a windswept desert into an oasis, from the snowy winter to a spring like setting of radiant cherry blossoms on a bright April morning.

It is having a new life, a new DNA and a new song in our hearts. For those who are searching diligently, God will bring them to the saving knowledge of His dear son. It is His word that none that come will be turned away. Why would you not come today dear man, dear woman. Come and prove His Word.

The Word [Jesus Christ] is now near us; it is in us, it is around us it is above us, it envelops us totally. It becomes a shining light unto our paths. A Light unto our path and a lamp unto our feet; the Scriptures says that it is. Can we trust the Word and must we not immerse ourselves in it. It is a treasure worth seeking after. A testimony from a user has and always will be of value to a prospective user or buyer of a good. I am testifying to the goodness of God right now and those who have endorsed this book are also testifying that what I write is their own experiences also. We can all declare that God is good and loving and He is ready to embrace us in his Son.

124 Having then accepted the Word, what manner of persons ought we to be as believers. Should we be like those speaking with fork tongues or should a hand shake be as weighty as a stamped document. Should we remain connivers and deceivers, employing the same deceptive tactics we used when we were in the world? When looking for a thief, can someone pass us by and know that they will not waste time here for it could not be us. When I worked for the TTC as an operator many years ago we were told not to clear the fare box ourselves if it got jammed with currency and tickets. If that happens, we are to call for a supervisor to come and clear it for us. When I called for one once, to have mine cleared, the supervisor I spoke to said: "Trevor *that does not mean you*, you go ahead and clear it." It means in all honesty, I am guilty as charged. I have been with Jesus, I am one of them. If we dare to be consistent then the world will not have to remind us of our status.

"Principles are deep fundamental truths, classic truths, generic common denominators. They are tightly interwoven threads, running

with exactness, consistency, beauty and strength throughout the fabric of life." Stephen R. Covey. Principle is like a well-tuned instrument in the hands of a proficient player. It is enjoyable and gives delight to the player and the listeners. Be determined to live as a principled person and you will have help living as one. Revise Micah 6:8 again. *"…And what doth the Lord require of thee, O man, but to do justly; and to love mercy, and to walk humbly with thy* God." Who else but the Christian fits this bill; no other, no matter how hard they try they will not come close.

I said to a brother in my adult Sunday School Class one morning. "If you came in and see me having breakfast in your kitchen one morning, your first reaction would not be to call the police but you would simply ask: *"How did you get in here."* And that not with a stern voice either but with a jovial one of course. If I laughed with him and did not tell him, he would still not call the police. The fact is that we are brothers and what is his is mine also. I wish we could be that close and yet we were called to be. We must live above the world and this worldly system. We are consecrated unto God not partially but wholly.

Paul said: *"Now I beseech you, brethren, by the name of our Lord Jesus Christ, that ye all speak the same thing, and that there be no divisions among you; but that ye be perfectly joined together in the same mind and in the same judgement."* 1 Corinthians 1: 10. Indeed this sounds like we are one happy family believing the one truth. There are too many minimalists under the umbrella of Christianity. Many think that just a little dabbing of Christianity is good enough and wants nothing to do with full indulgence in the work and development of themselves. Some will say it is not too good to be wholly holy. Christ said that however: *"Be ye holy for my Father is holy."* Holiness is definitely a goal that we should all aspire to.

The theory of the political system or the cosmos is that we Christians are bad for business so to speak, for we are oriented away from the world and its problems and that we try to avoid them by building in the future instead of here and now. That assumption is far from the truth as we are concerned about our planet in keeping it healthy and vibrant but we are simple not sending down deep125 roots here, rather we are more like tent dwellers; pilgrims or nomads in the broader sense. We live in constant expectancy that we could be called away to our permanent home any time.

However, that is not the case that we do not care about our planet that is a false assumption in that we participate fully in the care and preservation of the world. We more than any other recognize the command to care and replenish the earth and our thrust is not to enrich ourselves at the expense or at the dereliction of our planet. We are concerned citizens of this earth and happily make our contribution to its upkeep. We do not spurn our duty or responsibility to make good, our command from our Father, we are full participants in His creation.

If a careful study is made one would know that the many or most of the inventions to alleviate men's suffering were made by holy men and women of God. For the Christians are the more charitable of the two systems, it is they more than anyone else who would deny themselves to help others in need. It is they who will build and not tear down, help and not prevent, stand back and not usurp for gain. It is uswho will work with our Maker to create better and more satisfying systems of governance. Christianity has been a liberating force and an equalizer of mankind throughout the ages. It is an anomaly where it is practiced. The inhabitants everywhere feel it when it touches them. Life is injected into a community where the Christians touch; everyone can attest to this fact.

The world understands the idea of happiness in fundamentally materialistic and political terms. These are the pragmatic fields or dimension they seek to embrace more than anything else. Logically, there is a fundamental disjoint between how humans live and how we ought to live. The emphasis or proclivity is toward the wrong things. The emphasis is placed on transient objects while neglecting the spiritual or unseen. The world and the spiritual are at loggerheads and should be anyway, as our aims are different. Christ warns the Christian not to be friendly with the world and risk being the enemy of God.

Perhaps to suggest Plato's transcendental perspective where the distinction between the real world and the dimly lit cave of our embodied existence are at odds with each other is lost to the world. How else should it be anyway; without a clear distinction between the worldly and the spiritual, the transition would not be evident. As night and day are quite distinguishable so must the worldly and the spiritual.

CHAPTER 20

THE CERTAINTY OF THE PROMISE

The dawning of the age has already appeared with the first fruit Jesus Christ bursting forth from the grave to claim mastery and victory over death, that dreaded monster. Who can deny that such an event126 is not the foreshadowing of the great event spoken of in 1 Thessalonians 17 & 18. "For the Lord himself shall descend from heaven with a shout, with the voice of the archangel, and with the trump of God: and the dead in Christ shall rise first. Then we which are alive and remain shall be caught up together with them in the clouds, to meet the Lord in the air: so shall we ever be with the Lord." The promise of the resurrection is guaranteed by the triumph of the crucified Savour over death and that promise is signed and sealed on our behalf. We need not worry or hesitate to believe that truth for it is fully established that Christ rose from the dead. There is a cloud of witnesses as the bible declares.

It is amazing how many legends have been handed down and lives on from generation to generation and when it comes to the historical fact of Christ rising from the dead, there is a block. Some would rather believe that Christ's body was stolen. Of course, those who believe this lie remain in the congregation of the dead. There will not be that glorious resurrection for those who deny or refuse to believe the resurrection of Christ except to be raised to damnation. They wonder in the valley of indecision all their lives and live without the certainty that life is even real. The reality of our existence is settling in on many, even as I write these words. Our world is being shaken violently minute by minute and it is only the deaf who will not hear or heed the warning. God is speaking to our world and sin persists but in all of this, He stretches out His hand still. He beacons us to come and live.

There are two promises and they are made to all of mankind. One is death and the resurrection and the other is the Judgement. Your constitution and stamina does not matter, how strong and vigorous one is, the time comes when death knocks and we must answer. And after that we are helpless. Whether we be incinerated or buried in a ton of concrete after death, we will be raised again to face the judgement. We will have no say in this matter, we will be brought up for questioning and we will answer according to the deeds done in the body; whether they be good or evil. Need I say more here? God help us to see our plight without Christ as our advocate before God. *"If the righteous can scarcely be saved then where shall the sinner and the ungodly appear?"* 1 Peter 4:18. This portion of Scripture is scary I believe. If ever a portion is scary I find that this tops the list. My God, if after God's righteousness is imparted to us we barely made it in to the Kingdom how then will the ungodly and the sinner fare. I shudder to think.

Read my book, read my mind

Having entered the Kingdom, it is now my privileged responsibility to enlarge it. Is this statement apt to me alone or to everyone who indeed has entered it? To those of us who are in, God has enlarged our capacity to understand and indeed has enlightened us with wisdom so that we may live and act 127 prudently in all matters. We are now the great philosophers in the know. We are the truth bearing generation of this world. Now are we clothed in our right minds and can discern right from wrong, peer into the future and see coming events. Now for the first time in our lives, are we enlightened citizens. It would seem without boasting that we are on top of our game and in control of ourselves as never before.

Daniel 12:3 declares: *"And they that be wise shall shine as the brightness of the firmament; and they that turn many to righteousness as the stars for ever and ever."* God is now saying lend me your ears, and I will open your eyes, you that are mine so that I might reveal to you things which are about to come upon the earth that you be not caught up in them unawares. Be ready and not be found wanting like the five foolish virgins when I come. The message to the saved is as profound as that to the unsaved. To the saved, we are commanded to work in His vineyard and to the unsaved the message is to repent. We were not saved to be put on the shelf and wait for His second coming. We have a part to play in the Kingdom and in His vineyard. We must be soul winners; winning souls is our responsibility, all of us, not just for a select few and from the pulpit only.

When I was a Life Insurance Consultant, I did not go and sit in the office all week listening how to motivate clients and close policies and draw my pay come Friday evenings. Of course not, the work is in the field. You will have to go out and find clients and close businesses. You do not do this for one week but for as long as you last in the business you have to be a closer. Closing is the Life Insurance means of income and the source of our pay. I often compare winning souls to Life Insurance, in that you cannot last without closing or producing a certain amount of business for your office. Yet as part of the Kingdom of God many of us have no idea that we are all soul winners. We are to witness day in and day out. Of course, the very aroma that emits from our conversations and convictions must be a witness whether we use the Name of Jesus or not.

I heard a Church sister said one day that the only people she interacts with are the Christians so there was no an opportunity for her to witness. She is already in heaven and does not know it, if that is her attitude. We are now the light of the world and must shine to dispense the darkness. We must be a constant witness and when necessary use words to draw the ungodly in. God does not know one sinner that He did not die for; there is not one which He would turn away who comes in repentance. God is still in the business of saving souls and we are his agents. What further use have we then after we are saved if not to enlarge the Kingdom. If not, He might as well take us home as soon as we are saved.

People are worshipping, and people are attached to the things they worship; the fact is that many are backing the loosing horses. They have not yet learned the secret of winning. Many religions seem prosperous and attractive and not so much that there is a truthful message but that it suits its worshippers. It suits them because they are comforted more in their sins than they are disturbed by the messages. In many of the services you will come away with your plans to sin all intact as when you went 128 in. It will not make a difference to the conscience or the soul that you have been preached to because the sermon justifies what you are already doing rather than condemning it. Such places would rather be counting bodies than souls. They will tell you that I am alright and you are alright for God loves everyone. If your faith does not change your behaviour and action it will not change your destination either. It is therefore false and you cannot afford to continue in a false religion except that that person who does is a fool.

You alone are responsible for your soul. You have to give an account to God as we have heard two pages ago. Get out of the dead churches and link up to a Church with connection to Heaven so that when the roll is called up yonder you will be there. Don't gloss over this sentence as though it is not important and think that you have time to make right. This might be your last chance to make right with your Maker. I am pleading with you because I know that everything I write here is factual.

It is a certainty that such a preacher will meet his congregation again but he will not be able to offer a word of comfort because they will need comforting themselves. They, like those whose souls they have soothed will be in a hot place, a very hot place indeed. Proverbs 17:15 tells us: "He that justifieth the wicked and he that condemneth the just, even they both are abomination to the Lord. Many times both ideologies are embraced by the same person. They condone sinful acts and condemn or hate the person who speaks out against them. They are both living in the congregation of the dead, you can be sure of that.

God loves you to the point where He is reaching out to you and does not want you to go to the wrong place. He will not delight in you going to Hell. He has made every provision for you to secure a place with Him and He is trumpeting it everywhere so that you might hear and turn. Will you? Don't you ever believe that He doesn't love you even though you are wayward now? He has made provision for your rescue and survival but you will have to hold the life line when it is thrown out to you. On the other hand, never believe that you are a missing spoke in the wheel and that it will not function without you.

When a couple takes up an offering of one US Dollar from his village and walked for ten hours and a bus ride for another four hours to deliver it to a pastor who preaches the Gospel, acknowledging that such a Gospel has given them eternal life, which they never knew existed and they would never have, except someone told them; then you know that the Word of God is effective. It is changing lives, only that in some places like the wealthy nations of the world we are too busy playing with our expensive toys to listen to that Word. How very sad, for there will be a reversal at the end. Men and women will throw up their hands in disgust at their folly when they have found out that all their efforts amounted to zero. It all goes up in flames in the end.

The only things of lasting value are those done for Christ, such as this grateful couple's sacrifice of love.

Christ was here and they spat on Him and crucified Him but that was only the first round. The second round is still to come. That second round is His from the sound of the bell: Revelation 6: 15-17 states: *"And the kings of the earth, and the great men, and the rich men, and the chief captains, and the mighty men, and every bondman and every freeman hid themselves in the dens and in the rocks of the 129 mountains; 16 And said to the mountains and rocks, Fall on us and hide us from the face of Him that sitteth on the throne and from the wrath of the Lamb: "For the great day of His wrath is come and who shall be able to stand?"* That is the question, who shall be able to stand before the Lord to give a defence; No one. The books will be opened and everyman will hear his sins read as if they were just committed. Their knees will shake and as the saying goes, they will not have a leg to stand on. It is then that every knee will bow and every tongue confess that He is Lord. And who shall resist; no one. The Lord has spoken. If every person reading this sentence right now, drop everything they are doing and abandon it all and follow Christ, they will have done an immeasurable favour to themselves for all eternity. Nothing here is worth hanging onto, I can assure you. It is vanity and vexation of spirit; it will come back to haunt you if you neglect the salvation which is offered.

After acquainting oneself with these portions of scriptures, then who would not tremble unless they consider this to be as some say scaremongering. If you still believe in a God of mercy but not a God of justice, then you will not repent. This is exactly why you will bear His wrath because you do not think that He is just and will give everyman what they deserve. *"Be not deceived, God is not mocked for whatsoever a man soweth that shall he also reap."* Galatians 6:7. You are sowing now and to whom are you sowing, the world or to God? Remember, wherever your heart is there will your treasure be also.

Each person will inevitably follow their treasure. Will your treasure be like an inflated balloon against a pin? Or will it be able to withstand the fire; substantive and indestructible? The day of reckoning is coming and it is upon us even at the door; the signs are all around us. To ignore the word of God is to solidify your fate, it is ignoring God Himself and most definitely the God of the Word will on that great day shun you also. You will hear "Depart." He has already said that He will have no pleasure in declaring those words but you have asked that Christ's blood be upon your heads. You now will have gotten your well-deserved reward. You have chosen and God has spoken and it is done according to His justice.

The summer has come and the harvest is past. The books are closed, time is no more, eternity rolls and the sentence is fixed for that duration: " *Eternity.*"

The Cosmos and the Spiritual

Every movement requires a balance; we need two feet to walk, two hands to manipulate things properly, two sections of the brain to think properly and to reason, the night and day to balance our activities and two spheres of vision to live successfully. We are not one dimensional; we are at least two dimensional. The good and the bad, belief and unbelief and these are balances for our lives knowing or unknowingly.

Let us consider the Cosmos: (An ordered system of ideas) where men's intellect reigns supreme. He states that the world came into existence by the theory of the big "Bang." A convincing argument, especially when he was there with his camera to capture the event. He projects the event on his

130 panoramic screen and who can doubt it. I met a man in the Pocono Mountains in Pennsylvania in the USA and as I witnessed to him he countered with the big bang theory. He was in awe. He was convinced after seeing the event on the screen.

Such is man's ordered system and he is gaining ground. He is sweeping the world with his ideas. He is playing god. He sets himself up as god, assuming of course that that is the end of the story. Remember that he is projecting round one of a long fight. The outcome is fixed but he does not know it, so he thinks he will win the bout but he is wrong. He will struggle to stay on his feet all throughout the fight and in the end be knocked out unconscious; carried out on a stretcher never to recover. This is our destiny without God.

I am amazed and amused at the same time at how they come on as brilliant specimens and are playing little gods and how soon they exit the scene and we fight to remember what they stood for or looked like. Some of us would even be frightful of their faces for they are so fierce, doing what they do best and purporting to be of the essence and substance of invincibility. Man in essence is vanity, like the vapour that appears for a little while and then disappears without a trace. That is the essence of man.

They come on the scene out of University, crowing like a peacock with their chest high, philosophising their own paradigm, a new idea which they fashioned after their professors but the first act of philosophy is loving God and submitting to His Lordship. Therein is a person effective when they humble themselves before their Maker as the transcendent Being; the one to whom every knee will bow and every tongue will confess that He is indeed Lord.

At dinner one evening during the Easter break as we sat around the dinner table at my sister's place in Mississauga discussing religion, one young man pulled out his I pod and read from it. He wrote that if God was sovereign and knew all things then why did He allow sin to enter the world. When we begin to question and not accept things as they are then we make ourselves gods. Augustine said that if we can wrap out minds around all things then we would be God ourselves. God's knowledge transcends all things and we are the created beings, we are the clay and He is the potter and the clay cannot question the potter's actions. Sometimes I wonder at what stage did we get so bold as to question God's actions.

As we dissect that question we realize that God did not create sin. God simply gave Adam a choice. God made a stipulation as to what Adam can and cannot do and through the prompting of Satan he overstepped his boundaries. A simple thing it seemed but look what Adam got us into because of his disobedience. He subjugated the whole human race into sin, the most destructive force the world has ever known. We have all felt the ravages of sin in our lives and in our societies. We have felt it in our homes, at businesses and in the market place, it is everywhere playing havoc at every corner. Adam did get us into hot water. The answer to this young man's question "Why did God allow sin" is a not a valid one. Adam and not God brought sin into the world. Sin is not a hard thing to commit; it is simple and even a child commits sin just by disobeying.

God who is the Creator has the authority to make the rules. This is what you can do and this is what you are not to do and Adam did what he was told not to do and as such plunged the whole human race into sin. Sin is simple disobedience and that is all he did, disobeyed God. Adam experimented and men

131 are doing the same thing every day and will until the Lord appears again. As we consider the first half of the equation we will have to approach it with a quiet and humble attitude. We have to approach it with a contrite spirit and a desire to learn and understand the world we occupy. Anyone who is slightly curious about their life will ask questions as to what is the purpose of our existence and so on. How did we get here and where are we going from here. Is this all there is? This is a likely question we ask all the time and the answer is within us. There is a sea of knowledge around us attesting to the great fact that this is not half of what there is. Just as we are discovering that our earth is only a speck in this vast Universe; so are our lives. Our time here on earth is

only a speck in relationship to eternity where we will make our next stop and take up permanent residency.

Many approach the bench with a pedantic attitude, wanting to engage the world in conversation but to no conclusive end. They only want to be smart. They want to win the argument and move away from the discussion as the wise guy. They approach the bench with preconceived ideas and do not want to be instructed any further and although the truth stares them in the face, they will not see it. They fly the "Agnostic" flag and hope that, that too will get them leniency at the judgement day but they are so wrong. God is no respecter of persons. It is the Word which will judge us. He will open the books and say:"What did the book say you smart Alex, was it not clear enough?" Then you begin to stutter; *"But, but, but"*"Get out of my sight I never knew you!" God will reply. This dismissal will be their end.

We now move toward the bedrock of our civilization and our existence and that is the Spiritual. It is this dimension that is more important in the course of our existence. Is there a God who created all things and if so, are we responsible to Him for our behaviours. Is there a reporting at some time in our lives and so on? If so how do we know of these things? The Bible or the Scriptures is the Book which reveals the heart of God and the state of man and our destination and so on. Through the Scriptures God's plan is revealed in Jesus Christ who is the central figure in understanding God and creation.

The Church is left by Jesus Christ and must be internalized as a distinct community, a body if you may of insights and wisdom; believing the scriptures as a volume of testimonies and eyewitness accountsof the workings of God. We cannot fathom the depths of our destiny but must rely on the scriptures as our guide in assisting us. An understanding as to our appearing on planet earth andour destination must be attained and dealt with now while we are alive and sane. Having realized our position and coming to grips with these questions and having settled them satisfactorily, then we can proceed with our lives and begin to live as free and responsible human beings. We simply cannot gloss over these relevant questions, we must answer them or find the answers for them.

"For why will ye die" when such a provision for our comfort and prosperity is already provided for us through the death and resurrection of Our Lord and Saviour Jesus Christ. We need to have our questions answered and we can have them answered clearly and definitively when we approach the source with a heart to learn. The Scripture is unambiguous about our whereabouts. The scripture will tell us clearly where we are right now, our standing with our Creator and our future in relationship to His plans for this earth. He has a plan and to know it is wisdom.

132 The mockers and the scorners and the revisionist have been around since creation and they have gotten their rewards and are certainly not enjoying it and if you reading this account want to join the line with them you are free to. God himself will not forcibly let you change your mind. He has given you the offer of Salvation in His son the Lord Jesus Christ but will you take it? That is the question. Will you take it? The Word says: *"If today you would hear His voice harden not your heart."* Psalm 95:7. Today is the day of salvation; today and not tomorrow. Tomorrow might be too late, for the Spirit of God might not linger with you then.

When we stress the importance of coming to God through His book the Bible, many say we condemn them but of course we would respond that we do not, it is God's word which marks the line of demarcation. It is His word which separates the sheep from the goats, the believer from the unbeliever. So many are cut to the bone when you draw the line clearly between the believer and the non-believer the saints and the sinners. You define the end of both, and that hurts. Many see themselves good enough for heaven without accepting Christ as Saviour. They do not want to be the sinner and they are not the saints for they will not fully commit. Would not everyone want to have a safe and comfortable dwelling place and yet they want to live in two worlds; the cosmos and the spiritual; wanting only a little dabbing of spirituality and no more. Christ says we must take up our cross and follow Him and those looking back are not fit for the Kingdom. Lot's wife was turned into a pillar of salt after she looked back at Sodom when it went up into a conflagration.

When we witness with authority and confidence many are turned off and refer to us as arrogant but are we. If we plead with a person and desiring that they turn from their ways and trust our Saviour that we know as the only way, then that is not arrogance but compassion. Salvation is not something I want or we want to keep for ourselves only, no, it is enough to cover the whole seven or eight billion people and remains untouched still. Pointing out the danger that awaits a sinner is our business and the rebuttal that comes our way is but a small price to pay if we are rejected. Let us then be up and doing, seeking a heart for the task.

Many Christians seem to know a lot about God and His word but do we believe the Word. Do we even believe God? Just as in the garden of Eden the Devil asked Eve: *"Did God say this?"* Many are questioning God's word even as they read it. They want to put their own spin on it. I say we must believe God and His word and humble ourselves before Him and ask for wisdom in understanding what we do not grasp fully or readily. He will increase the depth of our understanding as we pursue His word.

God has spoken and I tremble at His word. As such I bowed in humble adoration before Him and ask for His forgiveness and Grace and I receive it. Today I sing the refrain of E.E. Hewitt.

Singing I go along life's road,
Praising the Lord, praising the Lord,
Singing I go along life's road,
133 For Jesus has lifted my load.

Will you join today that great throng which will be praising their Maker and Redeemer on that triumphant day when He returns to put all unrighteousness under subjection? Will you, will you?

One can joke about what might happen if ones house caught fire but if one day it were on fire in earnest, things will not be funny anymore. The fear that will grip you will be like no other you have experienced before. Come unto me the Lord Jesus cried and I will give you rest. Do you want that rest? It is in no other than the Lord Jesus Christ and you would better believe it. Do not wait and see. Why am I so dogmatic about this Christianity because I have spoken to many who have come from other permanent religions to embrace Christianity as the very truth they have been searching for all their lives. They worshipped in a quasi-religion and knew while they were there that it was false. It could not satisfy; it is like drinking sea water, for it will not quench your thirst. They all know the truth when they have experienced it and that truth rests only in Jesus Christ.

A great misnomer in our day is that if one knows some of the things which are written in the Scriptures they call themselves believers. Believers are those men and women, boys and girls who have the witness of the Spirit of God that Jesus is Lord and they worship Him as such. These are the saints of whom Paul speaks; they are the sanctified ones whose names are written in the Lamb's Book of life. They are the ones whom the spirit of God bears witness to, that they are His children. We no longer believe, we have come a far way from believing; now we experience it. It is our experience that He lives and that He lives in us; He moves and directs our actions and our daily activities. He is now Lord of our lives. End of story.

One great mind has said that trying to understand God is tantamount to a little child at the sea side digging a hole in the sand and filling it up with sea water with a bucket, he is diligently making his trips to and fro and someone comes along and asks: "*What are you doing child?*" "*I am emptying the ocean in* this hole." This is a comparison of our efforts to understanding the Omniscient God. It cannot be done and our best efforts fail in understanding the Great God. Our finite minds cannot fathom all that there is to know about God. We humble ourselves under His mighty hand and trust Him to see us through this maize.

The ungodly asks so many ridiculous questions about God, not hoping to get an answer, for we are fallible and can only give according as we have been enlightened by what is written. We are not left to ponder and wonder what things are beyond our realm of thinking and reasoning, we are given numerous examples and illustrations in the form of parables; simplifying things or bringing them down to our levels so we can ruminate on them. In Matthew 13:44 the Lord Jesus Christ gives us such an illustration of the Kingdom of God; one of ownership and possessing something of value which we all are anxious and happy to embrace. This is an addition to other parables he told of the Kingdom of heaven. He said: "*Again the kingdom of heaven is like unto treasure hid in a field, the which when a man hath found, he hideth, and for joy thereof goeth and selleth all that he hath, and buyeth that field.*" 134 In this parable we have a prospector searching for treasure; treasure of the highest value; treasure he can own and hold and value as worthwhile, wholesome and priceless. He owns many valuable treasures and know that what he has is not the ones he desires; in as much as he treasures them. He longed still for one more, or another he knows to be the pick of the crop so to speak. He knows that it is out there and he will find it, he is confident. His search has paid off because one day in his search he has discovered it. We are not told how long he was out searching but we can speculate that in his profession as a prospector he became a diligent searcher and perhaps developed his skill over many years. However, this is his day of discovery. This is his crowning day; he has finally stumbled upon the treasure he sought for so long. This is a special day, it is pay day and his efforts have paid great dividends.

The parable says: *"For joy thereof goeth and selleth all that he hath, and buyeth that field."* No, he did not add the old field to his wealth but sold it. Compared to this treasure, all his other treasures or possessions were substrata; they were not worth holding unto anymore. When one finds Christ by faith, they do not keep the idols and trinkets that held mystical meanings and charms to that believer and then tack Christ to the list. Now Jesus is enough and He is all that one needs. In Him are all the treasures of wisdom and knowledge. He is life, and joy and peace and everlasting life and the list is inexhaustible. We will be rejoicing for all eternity, for such a find; the Lord Jesus Christ. Christ as Lord is not added to our beliefs but replaces all other beliefs. He is elevated to first place in our lives and that is it. He is now our all in all.

I have heard some say, "You must have Jesus" as though there was some truth and urgency to it, yet they themselves are bowing down to idols every day. I told a man one day that he only tacks the name Jesus at the end of all the other saints and whomever he worships, just in case they do not come through, and then Jesus is there. The story we just read is that Jesus is the treasure of great price and all others are inferior to Him. He is Lord of all or not Lord at all. In the New Testament, the new believers burned their idols and put an end to those useless symbols once and for all.

Many call the name Jesus and worship other gods, how false can one get. They say you must have Jesus and bow down to idols. They use the name as a backup just in case the other gods do not come through for them. It is likened to carrying a spare tyre and a jack in your car just in case you get a flat. To many religions, Jesus has become that spare tyre and nothing more. Not many so called Christianssee Jesus as the deity He really is. They give Him only a passing glance, He might be the person some say He is but I think he was only a man. Some read the Bible and yet believe that Jesus had an earthly father, I have heard that said:"He must have an earthly father." That makes God's word untrustworthy when it states that Jesus was born of a virgin. Some equate Him to a teacher and others a prophet and link him with some mysterious prophets and so on. If you the reader does not recognize and worship Him as Lord, God and Creator, then you shall make your bed with those who dwell in darkness and in the congregation of the dead. These are not Trevor Turner's words but God's.

For your sake, it is worth it to divest yourself of all and follow Him. It has been done in the past and it continues to be a regular occurrence where men and women having found this Treasure are giving up all

135 to follow Him. It is only after having this Treasure that one is fully fortified, fulfilled with a magnificent future looming as large and as substantial as Mount Everest ahead. There is nothing to compare and this is the experience of one who is a part of that Kingdom. The promises of God are sure and certain and pure, please embrace them.

CHAPTER 21

THE ALL MIGHTY "WORD"

This four letter *"Word"* is mightier than all the neutron bombs and nuclear armaments put together. Its force is mightier than all the mighty waterfalls and hydro dams combined; it is the mightiest of all forces. It is a force which is established in the highest courts of heaven and it is one which we all will bow and submit to. It is everlasting and unchangeable. No one is immune to it. We will all be judged by it. It matters not whether you know it, believe it, heard it or respect it. Its liberating effect has been the central theme of man's enlightenment and freedom from time immemorial until the summation of all things; it will be the one constant which will never lose its power. Its cleansing power stands like the mighty ocean ever rolling and cannot be harness. The Word is the power of God unto salvation. It alone has the power to cleanse and make us whole. We would better get to know and respect it in all its facets.

A broken people we are, thus the need for the Word. The Word has been given to do its job in our lives and if neglected, we stand unfulfilled and unclean. The Word washes and renders us clean, clean enough to enter into God's presence. It will in the end be the judge of all mankind. Reverence the Word.

Christian brothers and sisters; love the Word, read the Word and live the Word. Unsaved person, do not mock and be irreverent to the Word, it will play a mighty part in your eternal welfare. In John 12:48, Jesus delineated the power of the Word in this statement. "He that rejecteth me, and receiveth not my words, hath one that judjeth him: the word that I have spoken, the same shall judge him in the last day." In my witness to people I hear that the word is manmade; written by men and not by God. Those are they who know little about or of the word of God. They are experts on the word and read little or none of it. They haven't the slightest inkling of the importance and weight of the Word of God.

In Psalm 119:89; *"Forever O Lord thy word is settled in heaven."* Does this passage reads like a statement that we think needs explanation or that we can trample under foot. Does it read like it needs further clarification or should we make an appeal for a less rigorous and intransigent dogma. Cain in his

136 dealings with God thought that God was too rigid by demanding an animal sacrifice so he brought out of convenience a fruit offering but it was rejected. God has spoken and we would do well to listen and conform. It is only when we see God as Isaiah did, will we be humbled and see ourselves as unworthy and vile. Only when those two spheres hit us; the Holiness of God and our unworthiness will we be ready to submit to God.

Everywhere and all throughout history men fight to minimize the word. They seek to lessen its power and make themselves greater than the word. God, they say is a benevolent God and will not do as he says he will. He is too merciful and will wink at their unbelief. That might have been so in the past but not now when we have the word. If you are reading this sentence or passages and believe you fall into that category you are dead wrong. You now have a responsibility to enquire about the Word and live by it or you will be judged by it. Acts 17:30 states: *"And the times of this ignorance God winked at; but now commandeth all men everywhere to repent."* We are now in the dispensation of grace where the Word dwells among us and as such we are without excuse, thus the command to repent. If you refuse the warning and the pleadings from the Father then you will have sealed your own doom. Need I say more?

"Peace" The possession of the Saints

Peace, the forte not of the strong, the brave, the wealthy; not of the intellectual but of the Saints. Peace a legacy given to us by our Redeemer the Lord Jesus Christ. The gift which passeth all understanding is not something worked up or imagined, it is a possession peculiar only to the redeemed and we say; "Glory to God for His unspeakable Gift." When the world trembles in its boots we can still have a good night's sleep because of this impartation. We do not sing about peace like a river glorious but we live like that glorious river because we possess that peace which flows out of our inner beings like that glorious river.

What do we possess as a consequence of the peace which we have? We have strength, stability and confidence. Ephesians 6:10. "Finally, my brethren, be strong in the Lord and in the power of His might." When we get in our cars and turn the keys, we depend upon the power of the engine to take the car we sit in wherever we want to go. We no longer believe that we are on our feet we know that there is power under the hood to take us places. That is the sole purpose of the car. Be strong in the Lord is an exultation, an upbraiding a marching order to go forth in the battle and conquer in the power of God the Almighty One. Paul gave this exultation as a summation to duty, here he said in full: "Finally, my brethren, be strong in the Lord, and in the power of his might." Ephesians 6:10. The antecedent of this exultation is found in Ephesians 6:6. "Not with eye service, as men pleasers; but as the servants of 137 Christ, doing the will of God from the heart." Thus we go forth to labour with full confidence as servants, winning souls for Christ.

David Livingstone was severely criticised for being a servant in his role as missionary in Africa. He did not laud over the natives but love them, embraced them as equals and as such he was love more than any other missionary was ever loved. His life did more to win more people for Christ than we can imagine. When he died his heart was extracted and buried under a sycamore tree in what was then Rhodesia but runners carried his body from the interior to the coast to be shipped back to Britain for burial. Such was their love for him. Livingstone's heart was in Rhodesia figuratively and is still literally. His life was not one of pretence, he loved the people he served and literally gave his life in their service. His was a life of full commitment; one we would do well to emulate.

This is the principle Paul is emphasizing, that we be sincere men and women serving our fellow men. We must get down to their level and love them and that is love magnified. Christ lived by example: Walking the dusty streets, roasting his fish and breaking bread with his friends; walking and talking and laughing with them as they journeyed from one place to the other. Even if they did not quite get what his mission was yet, He knew who He was and condescended nevertheless to meet them or us at our deepest need. How often do we stop to talk to someone who might be burdened by a problem and we could just listen if we took the time to speak to them and lift that burden by giving a word of encouragement. Like Christ, we know our position and cannot be contaminated so we can feel free to witness to them.

If ever there was a battle cry in the Scriptures, this is it. The cry is to get out from our complacencyand get out in the field of battle and serve. Serving not to be seen by others and to be commended by the church so to speak but get behind the scene and get our hands dirty to serve others. Christ noticed how the Pharisees served and gave; they wanted commendation and recognition by men so that everything they did must be noted or they would not do it at all. Paul wants us to do the very opposite, of course;

Christ sanctioned this road also so that what we do, we do unto God and not so that man might praise us. Our services can also go unrecognized by the eyes of men but God knows the least of it.

Be strong in the Lord has all manner of connotations such as a propensity for weakness in the body of Christ. Paul saw this as a shortcoming of the believers then and I see it as one today. We have a lot of talk, strong on lifting up holy hands but short on exercising faith. He admonishes us here in verse 14; "Stand therefore, having your loins girt about with truth, and having on the breastplate of righteousness." This is a picture of fortitude, of solidarity and confidence. In short, this is knowing your way around. To the onlooker you might be in a maize but you know just where and when to turn to make your exit. You are not lost, you have the map quite plainly in your head. Would this be a picture of the Christian who through diligent pursuit knows the power of the resurrected Christ in his or her life. No longer floundering and living a beggarly life but one of supernatural strength with all the host of heaven behind him as his strength and entourage. How should we go wrong and live as defeatist instead of overcomers. We should not falter after having all the resources of heaven at our disposal.

138 "Let us be up and doing with a heart for any fate, still achieving still pursuing…" From A psalm of life; by Henry Wadsworth Longfellow. God has not given us the spirit of fear but of power and love, and of a sound mind. This is an overcoming spirit that now dwells within us, so let us use it. The victory is already ours, so let us therefore, walk in light of that victory. As for me, I am determined to exercise this power which is vested in me. I do not want to shuffle off into eternity as a defeated foe, coming in from battle, but to march out as a conquering soldier entering His presence with an abundant entry, expecting His "Well done" approbation.

Fickle man versus the Immutable God

Disappointments in our lives is our constant companion because man promises but God disappoints in that we have not the ability to carry out our promises all the time. We make promises according to our hopes and fulfill them according to our abilities. That is to say when we promise we believe in all sincerity that we will be able to fulfill those promises but circumstances are the determining factor ultimately. Quite often extenuating circumstances override and render our ability to fulfill those promises null and void. In such times, we can use the old maxim: The heart is willing but the flesh is weak and so it is with human endeavours. We do not have the ability to see everything through to the end for we are not in control of events. We only think we are but far from it. The million and one things that can go wrong to obstruct our wishes that we can only promise with one thought in mind; DV: Deo Valente: The Latin term which means God willing? If it is God's will, I will do so and so and that is all. We cannot definitively make and carry out a promise. Although the chances are good for carrying out a promise we nevertheless cannot be sure. On the other hand, the Almighty and Immutable God direct all the elements to work for Him. He does not nor can He fail to carry out a promise or a command. Man, beast and the elements are all bidding His command, we can do no less nor more than He directs.

We live as free agents in a deterministic world. We are in the bubble or sphere and God is outside. There goes our restriction and mobility, so far and no further can we go. When we believe wholeheartedly the foregoing then we begin to humble ourselves under His mighty hand and know that we are but limited creatures living and breathing His dictates. We have a certain latitude to exercise our freedom but we are not absolutely free to do as we please. The sooner we realize this fact the better off we will be. Of course many do not acknowledge this fact and live as though they were in charge of themselves and their destiny.

Let us consider one character of the Bible and see if what I say here has any validity. In luke 12: 19 Jesus spoke of a certain man who prospered and felt that he could relax and enjoy his wealth at last. "And I will say to my soul, Soul thou hast much goods laid up for many years; take thine ease, eat, drink and be merry. Verse 20. But God said unto him, thou fool, this night thy soul shall be required of thee…" This is a sobering statement told to us by Jesus himself as to how we should live. Our lives are at best very fragile and are held in the Master's hand. To acknowledge this fact and to live in this light is the purview of the wise man. This is living wisely when we live in light of the brevity of life and in sight

139 of eternity. Only then will we have power with self, with man and with God when we keep connected to the Vine, may God help us to be connected permanently.

Our calling an election sure 2 Peter 1:10: "Wherefore the rather, brethren, give diligence to make your calling and election sure: for if ye do these things ye shall never fail." This passage suggests to me that the Christian pathway is a narrow road and needs our uttermost attention to navigate it to glory. The diligence which is required of us is diametrically opposed to the careless living being adopted by many. It is said that it does not take much of a person to follow Christ but it takes all of that person. Following Christ is not a walk in the park. It takes a devoted consistent person, determined to suffer if needs be but to make it to the end come what may. It is a fact that without starting, one can never finish but many have fallen by the wayside after starting. God is looking for not just starters but finishers. Walking with Christ is a daily walk, not a periodic renewing of acquaintances. It must become a friendship and an intimate relationship. His disciples were His family, more so than his siblings. How else would they learn of Him? There was an intimacy that we cannot fathom and yet we too need to enter into such a relationship.

If there is no appetite for the Word of God which is the source of knowledge and wisdom then we will never reach our full potential in Christ and be of service in the Kingdom of God. What good is the word if we do not read it and meditate upon it? And if it does not change our behaviours and move our actions, otherwise it is of no value. It will be like the medicine which lies on the counter untaken, while the patient languishes and dies. Active participation in the community of believers is the process of the Christian's life, there is no escaping this fact. To be fulfilled and buoyant, one needs this connection for upward mobility.

"Be very sure your anchor grips the solid rock: This rock is Jesus." What use is the anchor but to secure the ship when it needs to be secured? Our God is good for all seasons; He is for good times and for bad times and He is an ever present God whose word we can trust. *I will never leave you He said nor forsake you.* These are His words and they are trustworthy, never ever to be broken. These are the fundamental truths, the bedrock of our faith as Christians; we have God's Word and we have learned to trust His it and in addition to all of this, He abides with us and in us. We have been made to trust Him through the Holy Spirit dwelling in us and because of this we abide in safety and peace. What more could anyone desire or ask for. We have it all and we must know it and bask in it.

I encourage you fellow travellers; press on toward the mark of the high calling of God in Christ Jesus. Press on and never relinquish the fight, for the time of our refreshing is near.

"Now unto Him who is able to keep you from falling, and to present you faultless before the presence of His glory with exceeding joy, To the only wise God our Saviour, be glory and majesty, dominion and power, both now and ever. Amen." Jude 1:24-25. Go in peace, go with God.

Yours, in Christ, Trevor.